VIRTUOUS
LEADERSHIP

An Agenda for Personal Excellence

VIRTUOUS
LEADERSHIP

An Agenda for Personal Excellence

BY ALEXANDRE HAVARD

 Scepter

About the Author

Alexandre Havard is the author of the Virtuous Leadership model and the founder of the Havard Virtuous Leadership Institute (*www.hvli.org*). Born in Paris, he is a barrister by profession having graduated from the René Descartes University, one of France's leading law schools, and practiced law in several European countries. He is now living and working in Moscow where he offers seminars in Virtuous Leadership to senior business executives and university students. His book *Virtuous Leadership* (New York, 2007) has been translated into 15 languages, including Chinese, Russian, French, and Spanish. Alexandre Havard is also the author of *Created for Greatness: The Power of Magnanimity* (Washington, 2011).

Permission to quote copyrighted material is grately acknowledged to publishers and authors as follows: Simon & Schuster for quotations from *The 7 Habits of Highly Effective People*, by Steven Covey, © 1995. Random House, Inc., for excerpts from *The Life of Robert Schuman*, by Mary Schuman, © 1965.

Cover and Text Design: Rose Design

© 2007 Alexandre Havard
Published by Scepter Publishers, Inc.
www.scepterpublishers.org
All rights reserved

Second Edition, 2014

ISBN: 978-1-59417-204-5

Printed in the United States of America

To my grandparents,
Madeleine and Artchil, Nina and Pavel

ACKNOWLEDGMENTS

It was my happy lot to be born to and raised by people of exceptional virtue. That may sound corny to people of modern sensibility, but it's true. I refer to family members, beginning with my excellent parents and their parents—immigrants to France from the Soviet Union. They were people of heart who lived magnanimity, humility, prudence, courage, self-control, and justice as naturally as they breathed.

This book reflects their influence and that of some of the world leaders of my high school and university years who inspired me by their sterling moral example. Aleksandr Solzhenitsyn stands out, although I could name others, such as Pope John Paul II.

I grew up in revolutionary Paris of the late '60s and early '70s. Support for Red revolution was ubiquitous among the educated and semi-educated alike. The pampered children of Paris' finest *arrondissements* knew what they wanted—Communism. Most rejected the corrupt and flabby Brezhnevite dispensation in favor of the rigors of Maoist maximalism. For them, it was all or nothing. Their enthusiasm for Communism was surpassed only by their utter ignorance of life behind the Iron and Bamboo Curtains.

Solzhenitsyn's *Gulag Archipelago* burst on this scene like a thunderclap. The book exposed its moral pretentiousness, not to say vacuity, and washed it away like a sandcastle at high tide. The Russian author's heroic witness to truth, his astonishing courage in the face of evil, and his attachment to Christian moral precepts—so bracingly counter-cultural— made him seem far more youthful and relevant and attuned to the needs of the times than those clueless students on the barricades. He will always be seen by posterity in Russia and abroad as a paragon of virtuous leadership.

The other great inspiration of my life—the greatest, in fact—has been a Spanish priest and saint of the Roman Catholic Church: Josemaría Escrivá, the founder of Opus Dei. He taught me that Christ's famous commandment— "be perfect as thy Heavenly Father is perfect" (Matthew 5:48)—was addressed to me and to each and every one of His followers for all time; that it means living by the human and divine virtues; that the personal excellence to which Christ calls all of humanity is achievable, even by me. Saint Josemaría devoted his life to helping his children achieve this noble objective. His teaching, his example, and his spirit inform this book from start to finish.

I should like to thank my dear parents for their selfless love and support. They contributed to the book in many ways, great and small.

A number of other friends and colleagues contributed their professional advice and assistance, and for this I thank them. These include Joe Villagran, Michael O'Brien, Radosław Koszewski, Oskari Juurikkala, Mark Hamann, Josemaría Camean, Lembit Peterson, isä Rudolf Larenz, Don Juan José Sanguineti, Don Horacio Antunez, Varro Vooglaid, Sardor Nasyrov, and Rodrigo Preciado.

Above all, I should like to thank Anthony Salvia, whose contribution to every aspect of this book was so profound as to make him its virtual co-author. To him, my endless gratitude.

Last but by no means least, I should like to thank John Powers, of Scepter Publishers, Kevin Lay, who first read the manuscript, (insightfully), to Tony Salvia who made painstaking efforts to improve the English, and Russell Shaw, who edited the final manuscript. I am also grateful to Siobhan Hardy, whose cover design is the last word in graphic urbanity.

Needless to say, responsibility for any and all errors and/ or shortcomings rests solely with the author.

CONTENTS

Don't flutter about like a hen, when you can soar to the heights of an eagle.

—JOSEMARÍA ESCRIVÁ, THE WAY, NO. 7

AUTHOR'S FOREWORD

A random incident, as beautiful as it was unexpected, comes to mind whenever I contemplate the greatness of the human heart, which is the sine qua non of leadership and the very subject of this book.

It occurred on a bus journey from Saint Petersburg to Helsinki on a bitterly cold winter's morning in 1992, not long after the fall of Communism. This was a time of plunging production, skyrocketing inflation, and rampant unemployment throughout the former Soviet Union. Elderly Russians found themselves in especially dire straits as inflation wiped out their already inadequate pensions. Many were reduced to collecting discarded bottles from waste bins for the deposit money. It was their only way to survive.

As the Finland-bound bus sped through Russia, I was struck by the contrast between the pristine winter landscape hurtling past my window and the less than edifying moral atmosphere on board.

The passenger in front of me was sloshed. He appeared to be comatose.

The passenger to my right thrust his hand into his pocket and came up with a crumpled pack of cigarettes. He regaled me with stories of a lost weekend of carousing, as he chafed at not being able to light up.

Much to his relief, our bus put in for a rest stop in front of the railway station at Vyborg, the last Russian city before the Finnish frontier. With the sun shining brightly on newly fallen snow, I bundled up against the cold and set out to explore the area around the station.

Presently I came upon an old lady rummaging through a large pile of refuse to find something she could use or sell or cash-in for the deposit. I reached into my pocket and came up with my few remaining rubles: "Babushka, please take these." She looked me straight in the eye and smiled radiantly, and I could see that she was younger than she appeared. Anxious not to miss the bus, I made my way quickly back to the station.

Just as I was stepping aboard, I heard a voice behind me. I wheeled around. It was the old lady trundling towards me as fast as she could, a beaming smile on her face and a bouquet of flowers in her outstretched hand. I accepted it. She left without saying a word.

We crossed the border and left my beloved Russia behind. I lay back, closed my eyes, and pictured her buying the flowers with money she so desperately needed for herself and with no certainty of finding me. I marveled at her absolute selflessness, her generosity of heart. I was overcome with joy, with a deep love for life, with a desire to convert, to purify my heart, to be better.

It is by no means unusual that a close encounter with goodness makes the soul take flight, as though it had sprouted wings.

In this book and in the seminars on Virtuous Leadership *that I give to audiences of widely different cultures and languages and religions, I strive to impart some of what the old lady of Vyborg imparted to me. Nothing is more satisfying for me than to see my readers and students and program participants conceive a new desire to grow in the daily, conscientious practice of the classical human virtues. When they grasp that leadership is service or, if you will, virtue in action, I can sense their souls taking flight, as if they had sprouted wings.*

INTRODUCTION

Leadership Is Character

LEADERSHIP IS ONLY SUPERFICIALLY about what we imagine. Hearing the word, we think of heads of state or government moving nations to action, captains of industry bringing products to market that change our lives, generals leading armies into battle. We suppose it to be an amalgam of ambition, charisma, cunning, know-how, access to money, and a gift for being in the right place at the right time.

These are talents and qualities and resources leaders can use to advantage, but none of them constitutes the essence of leadership.

Leadership is about character.

No, leadership *is* character.

There are those who think one must be born to lead— that some have a knack for it and some do not, that leadership is largely a matter of temperament combined with experience. Not everyone can be a Roosevelt or a de Gaulle or a Churchill, they think.

Nothing could be further from the truth. Leadership is not reserved to an elite. It is the vocation not of the few but the many.

Heads of state and schoolteachers, captains of industry and housewives, military chiefs of staff and health care workers—all exercise leadership. People expect them to do the right thing, to be men and women of character and virtue, to be motivated by a magnanimous vision for all those in their charge. And great is the disappointment when they fail.

The business scandals of our time invariably give rise to calls for increased government oversight, reform of corporate governance, and revision of codes of ethical conduct.

These things may have their place, but they miss the essential point. The perpetrators of corporate wrongdoing invariably know that what they are doing is wrong. And yet they do it anyway. This is a failure of character.

Dr. Martin Luther King dreamed of an America in which a man would be judged "not by the color of his skin, but by the content of his character."

What is the "content of character?" It is virtue, or, more precisely, the set of classical human virtues—above all, magnanimity, humility, prudence, courage, self-control, and justice—that are the subject of this book. It is my contention that leaders either strive to grow in virtue as surely as they breathe or they are not leaders. Life for them is a quest for personal excellence.

Virtuous Leadership *is for people who desire to have a grand purpose in their life. What purpose is grander than the quest for personal excellence?*

The book defines each of the classical human virtues most essential to leadership (Parts 1 and 2), examines how leaders grow in virtue (Part 3), demonstrates how virtues lead to self-fulfillment (Part 4), and considers the grandeur of the supernatural virtues of faith, hope, and charity and their impact on leadership (Part 5).

Virtuous Leadership: An Agenda for Personal Excellence emerges from the executive program of the same name, which I lead, and from the question participants invariably put to me, "What you say about virtue is all well and good, but I'm busy with work and family. How, in practical terms, do I achieve the 'personal excellence' of which you speak?"

The answer is in the book's final chapter, "An Agenda for Victory." There you will find a tried-and-true methodology for the achievement of personal excellence tailored to the needs of busy, professional people.

Before entering into a detailed consideration of each of the human virtues of greatest relevance to leadership, let us get our bearings by reflecting on some general observations about character, virtue, and temperament.

⁓

"It is character through which leadership is exercised,"[1] avers Peter Drucker, the preeminent management theoretician of modern times.

His professional confrere, Warren Bennis, concurs: "Leadership is not a superficial question of style, but has to do with who we are as human beings . . . The process of becoming a leader is much the same as the process of becoming an integrated human being."[2]

We acquire integrity and maturity through our own efforts. The very effort to acquire them is an act of leadership.

Leadership, therefore, cannot be temperament, because temperament is given by nature. One's temperament is phlegmatic or hot-blooded, for example, not because one chose it, but because that's the hand nature dealt.

Leadership can only be character.

Character is not forced on us by nature, however. We are not stuck with it. It is something we can shape and mold and

---

1. P. Drucker, *The Practice of Management*. Oxford: Elsevier, 2005, p. 155.
2. W. Bennis, *On Becoming a Leader*, New York: Addison-Wesley, 1989. Introduction.

strengthen, and as we do so, we achieve Bennis' centeredness, congruity, and balance.

We strengthen our character through the habitual practice of sound moral habits, called ethical or human virtues. In so doing, character leaves an indelible imprint on our temperament, which then ceases to dominate our personality.

Virtues are qualities of the mind, the will, and the heart that instill strength of character and stability of personality. They are acquired through repetition.

The four main human virtues as defined by Plato are prudence, justice, courage, and self-control. These are the so-called *cardinal* virtues, from the Latin word *cardo*, or "hinge." These are the virtues upon which all other human virtues hinge. Each of the *non-cardinal* virtues is bound up in and depends on one of the *cardinal* virtues.

In the *Book of Wisdom*, we read: "Wisdom teaches self-control and prudence, justice and courage, and nothing in life is more useful than these."[3] That the Old Testament mentions the four cardinal virtues shows that the Jews valued the wisdom of the ancient Greeks.

We must mention two other virtues—magnanimity and humility. Both are fundamental, though are not considered cardinal by tradition. For the ancient Greeks, humility depended on the cardinal virtue of self-control and magnanimity on the cardinal virtue of courage.

Virtues are dynamic forces—witness the word's Latin root, *virtus*, meaning "strength" or "power." Each, when practiced habitually, progressively enhances one's capacity to act.

Here is what each of the six virtues under consideration enhances the ability to do:

---

3. Wis 8:7.

- *Prudence:* to make right decisions.
- *Courage:* to stay the course and resist pressures of all kinds.
- *Self-control:* to subordinate passions to the spirit and fulfillment of the mission at hand.
- *Justice:* to give every individual his due.
- *Magnanimity:* to strive for great things, to challenge myself and others.
- *Humility:* to overcome selfishness and serve others habitually.

Virtues do not take the place of professional competence, but are part and parcel of it and substantially so. I might have a degree in psychology and work as a consultant, but if I lack prudence, I will have a hard time giving my clients sound advice. Perhaps I have an MBA and am a senior executive for a major corporation. Very good, but if I lack courage, my ability to lead in the face of opposition is already compromised. I may have a degree in theology and serve as a minister, but if I am devoid of magnanimity, I will stagnate as a person and as a believer, and will lead my flock into the same condition.

Professional competence entails more than the mere *possession* of technical or academic knowledge. It includes the capacity to use this knowledge well for some fruitful purpose.

Leaders are defined by their magnanimity and humility. They always have a dream, which they invariably transform into a vision and a mission. It is magnanimity—the striving of the spirit towards great ends—that confers this lofty state of mind.

But leadership consists of more than just "thinking big." A leader is always a servant—of those in his professional, familial, and social circle, his countrymen, and indeed the whole of humanity. And the essence of service is humility. Leaders who practice humility respect the innate dignity of other people, and especially of fellow participants in a joint mission.

Magnanimity and humility go hand in hand in leadership. Magnanimity generates noble ambitions; humility channels these ambitions into serving others.

Charisma in leadership stems from visionary greatness (magnanimity) and devotion to service (humility). Magnanimity and humility are virtues of the heart *par excellence*, giving leaders who possess them a charismatic touch. We must not confuse charisma with a gift for galvanizing the mob. "Leaders" who possess this dubious talent may generate short-term enthusiasm, but rarely confidence, and ultimately only derision and contempt. Mussolini is a case in point. Leadership is not demagoguery. It is about excellence sustained over the long term, even if the leader lacks a magnetic personality.

Magnanimity is under severe strain these days. Modern society's weird mélange of individualism and collectivism has spawned generations of small, self-centered people on the make. Humility has also seen better days. Modern culture holds this marvelous virtue—understood as service—in something approaching contempt. Until not too long ago, service was one of the loftiest words in our vocabulary; now it is an almost exclusively commercial concept. When we speak of service, we mean business services, remunerated services, the services (i.e., non-manufacturing) sector, and the like. We think of service as something you buy.

If magnanimity and humility—the essence of leadership—are virtues principally of the heart, the cardinal virtues of prudence, justice, courage, and self-control—leadership's bedrock virtues—are principally of the mind and the will. Prudence, the virtue specific to decision-makers, is the most important, since to lead effectively I need the capacity to make right decisions.

Virtue creates the space in which leadership occurs by instilling trust. Humility and prudence are vital here. This is because trust begins when others know I will serve them, which is humility, and ends when they discover I am unable to make right decisions, which means I lack the virtue of prudence.

If I replace humility with techniques of communication, I will fail as a leader. As Stephen Covey points out, "If I try to use human influence strategies and tactics of how to get other people to do what I want, to work better, to be more motivated, to like me and each other—while my character is fundamentally flawed, marked by duplicity and insincerity—then, in the long run, I cannot be successful."[4]

Leaders never resort to manipulation. Nor do they lead by exercising the *potestas*, or power, inherent in their office. Instead, they lead through *auctoritas*, the authority that stems from character. Those who lack genuine authority and succumb to the temptation to exercise unalloyed power are leaders in name only. In fact, they are non-leaders. This is a vicious circle: low authority leads to abuse of power, which leads to further erosion of authority ... and the path to authentic leadership is blocked.

Because virtue is a habit acquired through practice, I say leaders are not born, but trained. Not everyone can become president or prime minister or win the Nobel Prize for Literature or play center field for the New York Yankees. But everyone can grow in virtue.

Leadership excludes no one.

---

4. S. Covey, *The 7 Habits of Highly Effective People.* New York: Free Press, Simon & Schuster, 2003, pp. 21–22.

Leaders reject a utilitarian approach to virtue. It is not something they cultivate just to become better at what they do, although it is good to want that. They cultivate virtue first and foremost to become better people. *Aretē*, the Greek word for virtue, implies excellence of being, rather than excellence in doing.

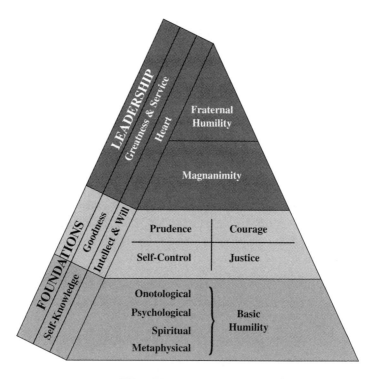

**THE VIRTUOUS LEADERSHIP
PYRAMID**

© A. Havard

PART I

GREATNESS AND SERVICE

Magnanimity and humility define the leader.

Magnanimity is the quest of the spirit for great things. He who strives for greatness and seeks to correspond to it is magnanimous. Magnanimity is rooted in a firm confidence in the highest possibilities of human nature.

Humility is the habit of living in the truth about one's metaphysical condition, and one's strengths and weaknesses. It is also the habit of service to family and friends, colleagues and clients, society at large, and indeed all of humanity. Humility fosters in leaders the ambition to serve unconditionally.

CHAPTER 1

Magnanimity
Striving Towards Great Things

> Leadership is the lifting of a man's vision to higher
> sights, the raising of a man's performance to a higher
> standard, the building of a man's personality beyond
> its normal limitations.
>
> —*PETER DRUCKER*

LEADERS ARE MAGNANIMOUS, high-minded, and conscious of their potential for greatness. Their dream is to conquer the summit of professional achievement and personal excellence.

The classical definition of magnanimity is *extensio animi ad magna*—the striving of the spirit towards great things. The Latin word *magnanimitas* derives from the Greek *megalopsychía*. Its opposite is *micropsychía*, which means pusillanimity or small-mindedness.

Small-minded men cannot even conceive of greatness. The notion that life has a high purpose is foreign to them. Ivanoff, the central character in Anton Chekhov's play of the same name, gives advice to a friend that anyone who dreams of being magnanimous would be well advised to ignore:

> "My dear friend, you left college last year, and you are still
> young and brave. Being thirty-five years old I have the

3

right to advise you. . . . Choose some nice, commonplace girl without any strange and startling points in her character. Plan your life for quiet; the grayer and more monotonous you can make the background, the better. . . . That is the pleasant, honest, healthy way to live."[1]

Leaders are magnanimous in their dreams, visions, and sense of mission; in their capacity for hope, confidence, and daring; in their enthusiasm for the effort required to bring their work to a successful conclusion; in their propensity for using means proportionate to their goals; in their capacity to challenge themselves and those around them.

Consider the example of the remarkable men who founded the European Union—Robert Schuman, Jean Monnet, Konrad Adenauer, and Alcide de Gasperi. They understood that the key to overcoming centuries of division and conflict and ruinous wars was *integration*—the fusion of national interests—rather than mere *cooperation*.

Robert Schuman, the French Minister of Foreign Affairs, saw Franco-German friendship as the fundamental precondition for European integration. This was magnanimous on his part, for having been a prisoner of the Gestapo in Nazi-occupied France, he had good reason to mistrust the Germans. Moreover, most Frenchmen continued to see Germany as a mortal rival and potential aggressor. Schuman was able to transcend the legacy of Europe's troubled past for the sake of the common good—the good of Europe as a whole and of France and Germany in particular.

As German Chancellor Konrad Adenauer observed: "The powerful and daring initiative of Robert Schuman was an act of extraordinary significance. . . . Thanks to his prudence and values, he laid the foundations for reconciliation

---

1. A. Chekhov, *Ivanoff*, Act I, Scene V. Kila, MT: Kessinger Publishing Co, 2004.

between our two countries and for the construction of a united and strong Europe."[2]

Dean Acheson, the U. S. Secretary of State, wrote in his memoirs: "Schuman possessed a vision of a united Europe in a day and age when it was difficult to have a vision in France of any kind."[3]

In 1960, the European Parliament unanimously declared Schuman the "Father of Europe," a title no one else can lay claim to.

Like Robert Schuman, Ronald Reagan had a vision that contradicted the main political currents of his time, above all his approach to dealing with Communism. Far from seeing Communism as a permanent feature of the political landscape, which the West had no choice but to accommodate, Reagan was determined to pave the way for its demise. He did so through his foreign and defense policies, but also by speaking the truth about the nature of the Soviet regime.

Reagan speechwriter Peggy Noonan observes: "He [Reagan] thought the truth is the only foundation on which can be built something strong and good and lasting—because only truth endures. Lies die. He thought that in politics and world affairs in his time there had been too many lies for too long, and that they had been uniquely destructive. And so his career was devoted to countering that destructiveness by speaking the truth, spreading it, and repeating it."[4]

When Reagan called the Soviet Union the "focus of evil in the modern world," and expressed his view that it would soon be flung onto the "ash heap of history," he was simply

---

2. See R. Lejeune, *Robert Schuman, Père de l Europe*. Paris: Librairie Académique Perrin, 1980, chapt. 21.

3. See R. Lejeune, *op. cit.*, chapt. 15. Translation by the author.

4. P. Noonan, *When Character was King, A Story of Ronald Reagan*. New York: Penguin Books, 2002, pp. 200–201.

speaking the truth as he saw it. Having the courage of his convictions, he acted to bring about results he felt were good for his country and, it should be noted, for the Russian people, who had suffered so much under Communism. Towards the end of his eight years in office, Reagan went to Berlin and called on Mr. Gorbachev to "tear down this wall." In short order the Berlin Wall fell, and Communism was relegated to the ash heap of history.

Similarly, Lech Walesa, the Polish electrician who founded the Solidarity labor union, made a signal contribution to positive political change in Poland and throughout Eastern Europe by insisting on giving words their real meaning. Communism preached social solidarity but ruled by means of repression. Communism claimed to represent the working class, but banned trade unions, collective bargaining, and the right to strike. Walesa chose to attach the real meaning to these concepts. He did not so much strike a blow against Communism as a blow for truth, a blow Communism did not survive.

As George Weigel points out: "What made Solidarity work was that millions of people, many of them non-Christian, committed themselves to living Christian values: the honesty that stood in sharp counterpoise to Communism's lies about everything; the courage that faced up to communist brutality; the fraternity that resisted communism's attempts to divide and rule."[5]

Cory Aquino, the President of the Philippines from 1986 to 1992, is another political visionary. Upon the assassination of her husband, the popular senator Benigno Aquino, Mrs. Aquino became the focus of opposition to autocratic president Ferdinand Marcos. With most Filipinos convinced

---

5. G. Weigel, *The Cube and the Cathedral*. New York: Basic Books, 2005, p. 129.

that the government had ordered her husband's death, Mrs. Aquino boldly announced her intention to challenge Marcos for the presidency in the 1986 election. The official vote tally declared Marcos the winner, but there was evidence of widespread fraud. Both candidates claimed victory and held rival inaugurations. Hundreds of thousands took to the streets in support of Mrs. Aquino in a notable demonstration of "people power." With the country united against him and the military refusing to intervene on his behalf, Marcos fled the country.

"I assumed the powers of the dictatorship, but only long enough to abolish it," said Mrs. Aquino years later. "I had absolute power, yet ruled with restraint. I created independent courts to question my absolute power, and finally a legislature to take it from me."[6]

Mrs. Aquino's vision was a moral one. She felt that it was her duty to strive for the common good and that this meant creating a just social order for each and every Filipino. She never accepted the idea of democracy for democracy's sake. "Without the right values in the people," she said, "a democracy is only a confederacy of fools."[7]

Mrs. Aquino was a singular example of sincerity, simplicity, and integrity in politics. She served for one six-year term and chose not to seek re-election. Long after she ceased to be President, Filipinos still looked up to her as a leader who united the nation.

Two leaders of the early twentieth century stand out as exemplars of magnanimity in action: Pyotr Stolypin, prime minister of Russia under the last Tsar, Nicholas II, and Karl von Habsburg, Emperor of Austria-Hungary.

---

6. C. Aquino, *address to the international student congress* UNIV, Rome, March 1993.
7. Ibid.

Pyotr Stolypin served as prime minister from 1906 to 1911. Easily the most distinguished of Nicholas' heads of government, Stolypin was the only one with a vision of how to put an end to the wave of terror and revolution that had been sweeping Russia for decades. His plan consisted of giving the Russian peasantry and working class a stake in the economic system, so that for the first time in modern Russian history they could benefit from the fruits of their labor. He called for the legal and administrative transformation of the empire. The keystone of his program was agrarian reform.

This was a risky and politically charged undertaking in a nation whose population was 80% rural. In Stolypin's time, socialists and conservatives alike felt an almost mystical veneration for the traditional village commune—a form of collective land-ownership by the peasantry. Socialists cherished the commune because they saw in it a precursor of their plan to socialize all of economic and social life. The conservative land-owning class, meanwhile, considered the village commune the very underpinning of the nation's social order and of its own power and influence.

Stolypin was by temperament, education, and political inclination a conservative, but being a prudent man, he was first and foremost a realist. He understood that the commune was morally unjust, economically inefficient, and the main cause of social instability. Imbued with an egalitarian spirit, the commune required that land be distributed more or less equally. It sought to make each member of the commune responsible for all; to this end it constantly redivided arable land. The individual peasant thus found it impossible to improve his lot and grew disheartened. In time, the peasant commune became fertile ground for revolutionary agitation.

Stolypin's agricultural reform program provoked the bitter opposition of the Socialists, who had no desire to see the Tsar carry out a successful reform to benefit the very constituency whose disaffection they sought to exploit. No less opposed were the powerful landowners, who feared an empowered peasantry would put an end to a centuries-old social system that was the source of their power. Fearing the wrath of the opposition, the Tsar backed away from his prime minister.

Had Russia adopted the Stolypin reform program, avers the great Russian writer, Aleksandr Solzhenitsyn, the program would have created an independent peasantry within twenty years and saved the nation from Bolshevism.

Instead, the program ended in defeat opening the path to Red revolution. Stolypin was alone in his struggle, but he never gave up. He carried on with his mission until he was assassinated in September 1911 by Dmitri Bogrov, a shadowy figure with links both to revolutionary terrorists and the Tsarist secret police.

Karl Franz Josef von Habsburg-Lothringen, the last Emperor of Austria-Hungary, ascended to the throne in 1916, two years after the outbreak of the Great War, at the age of 29.

Karl understood that his mission was to halt the conflict. "Since my accession to the throne," he said, "I have unceasingly tried to spare my nations the horror of the war, for the outbreak of which I bear no responsibility." Historian Warren Carroll, commenting on Karl's February 1917 peace initiative, calls it "by far the most genuine and unselfish peace offer by the head of government of a belligerent state in the whole course of the war." The famous French writer Anatole France wrote: "The Emperor Karl offered peace. He was the only honest man to occupy an important position during the war, but he was not listened to. . . . He had a sincere desire for peace, so everyone hated him."

In times of hatred, Karl was a man of peace who consistently made decisions on the basis of what was just. He forbade the use of mustard gas, the aerial bombardment of cities, and wanton destruction of any sort, including plunder on the part of the Austro-Hungarian armed forces. In April 1917, he learned of a plan of the German High Command to knock Russia out of the war by sending Lenin and other Bolsheviks, then in exile in Switzerland, back to Russia to foment revolution. Karl strongly opposed the plan and refused to allow the train carrying Lenin and his entourage to cross the Austrian frontier. Rebuffed, the German government sent the train through Sweden instead. Years later, the Empress Zita said her husband had refused to act toward the Russian people in a way that would be "unfair and irresponsible."

If more leaders had acted as he did, the twentieth century might have been radically different. Historians generally agree that the First World War gave rise to both Bolshevism in Russia and Nazism in Germany, which in turn gave rise to the Second World War and the Cold War.

On November 11, 1918, Karl was obliged to renounce the Austro-Hungarian throne. Three years later, after much suffering, he died in exile on the island of Madeira at the age of 34, leaving behind a widow, five sons, and three daughters.

Karl of Austria-Hungary may have failed in his mission—the spirit of evil was abroad in Europe as never before—but he succeeded magnificently as a leader. In this he resembled Stolypin. These were men of heart and vision—beacons of magnanimity in a dark age. Their example will inspire men of good will for generations to come.

Business, like politics, is a field for leaders, for men and women possessed of dreams and visions, and eager to carry them out. But because business is also about money, some perceive it to be tawdry and those involved in it self-serving. They believe it offers scant opportunity for personal greatness, although they understand that business is a socially useful activity because it gives us lots of things we need and want, from toothpaste to iPods.

Three hundred years ago the English pamphleteer Bernard Mandeville originated the popular misconception that business is a necessary evil, even though he perceived its social benefits. He claimed that *private vices* such as luxury, greed, and envy, lead to *public benefits* by encouraging enterprise: "Thus every Part was full of Vice/Yet the whole Mass a Paradise."[8]

In fact for many entrepreneurs and managers, business is not first and foremost about making money, but rather a vehicle for achieving personal and organizational greatness, for accomplishing something worthwhile and noble together with others. Mature business people are driven neither by personal financial gain nor by an obsessive desire to increase shareholder value. Profit is a necessary goal of business activity, but not its purpose.

Was John D. Rockefeller, who rose from being a clerk in a merchant banking house to be one of the world's richest men, a great man? Was Andrew Carnegie, who started out as a $1.20-a-week laborer in a Pittsburgh cotton mill, only to become the nation's foremost steel magnate, a great man? I think few people would say they were great. What we admire about these "entrepreneurial heroes" is not any particular vision, but the fact that they were self-made men—and little more. Rockefeller and Carnegie obviously had dreams, but

---

8. B. Mandeville, *The Fable of the Bees: or Private Vices, Publick Benefits*. Oxford: At the Clarendon Press, 1714.

they were not the dreams of genuine leaders. They had no mission, they had only a goal—to be their own boss.[9]

Carnegie wrote: "Is any would-be businessman . . . content in forecasting his future, to figure himself as laboring all his life for a fixed salary? Not one, I am sure. In this you have the dividing line between business and non-business; the one is master and depends on profits, the other is servant and depends on salary."[10] This is far from being a vision engendered by magnanimity; rather it is an apologia for arrogance.

Some would say it constituted magnanimity for these business magnates to give multi-millions to cultural and charitable institutions, but it comes closer to the mark to call it philanthropy. Philanthropy is a beautiful thing, but it is not the same thing as magnanimity, especially if one gives from one's surplus without making any personal sacrifice. Magnanimity is about more than writing a generous check; it is about the gift of one's very self.

By contrast, Darwin E. Smith and François Michelin stand as sterling examples of magnanimity in corporate life.

Darwin Smith was the mastermind of Kimberly-Clark's remarkable turnaround. When Smith took over the helm of Kimberly-Clark, a major paper manufacturer, the firm was on the ropes. The value of its stock had fallen by some 40% over the previous twenty years, as its principle business—the production of coated paper—had become an enterprise with low margins.

If Kimberly-Clark was in poor financial shape, the state of Smith's health was dire. Two months before being named

---

9. See R. B. Reich, "Entrepreneurship Reconsidered: The Team as Hero." in *Harvard Business Review*, May 1, 1987, p. 78.

10. A. Carnegie, *The Empire of Business*. New York: Doubleday, 1902, p. 192. Cited in "Entrepreneurship Reconsidered," *op. cit.*

CEO, Smith was diagnosed with nose and throat cancer. Nevertheless, he maintained a grueling work schedule, including commuting every week between the firm's Wisconsin headquarters and chemotherapy sessions in Houston. Although doctors gave him only a couple of years to live, he maintained this work routine for twenty years, most of them as CEO.

"Smith brought that same ferocious resolve," writes business guru Jim Collins, "to rebuilding Kimberly-Clark, especially when he made the most dramatic decision in the company's history: Sell the mills. Shortly after he became CEO, Smith and his team had concluded that the traditional core business—coated paper—was doomed to mediocrity. Its economics were bad and the competition weak. But, they reasoned, if Kimberly-Clark were to thrust itself into the fire of the *consumer* paper-products industry, world-class competition like Procter & Gamble would force it to achieve greatness or perish. So, like the general who burned the boats upon landing, leaving only one option (succeed or die), Smith announced the decision to sell the mills. . . . Sell even the mill in Kimberly, Wisconsin, and throw all the proceeds into the consumer business, investing in brands like Huggies and Kleenex."[11]

Wall Street lost no time expressing its lack of confidence. Kimberly-Clark stock continued its downward slide. Meanwhile, a chorus of journalistic naysayers predicted the firm's imminent collapse. But Smith did not waver. He proceeded serenely to implement his new vision, transforming a dying industrial giant into the world's leading paper-based consumer products company. Ultimately, the firm generated returns 4.1 times greater than

---

11. J. Collins, *Good to Great*. New York: Random House, 2001, pp. 17–18, 20.

the market average, far surpassing such rivals as Scott Paper and Procter & Gamble.

Reflecting from retirement on his performance, Smith observed, "I never stopped trying to become qualified for the job." Telling in its humility, the remark belies the extraordinary leadership qualities Smith possessed in formulating a bold strategic vision and making it work. To turn one's back on 100 years of corporate history and risk all on the thorough transformation of the business requires outstanding vision and true leadership.

François Michelin, the former managing partner of Group Michelin, transformed his company and the entire industry with his visionary plan to bring the technologically sophisticated radial tire to market. He firmly believed that business was more about creativity than the bottom line.

Not content to continue manufacturing tires by the tried and true method, Michelin bucked the conventional wisdom of industry experts, whom he called "old fogies in their mid-twenties who preferred to extrapolate curves rather than put their faith in human imagination."[12]

An accomplished engineer as well as a businessman, Michelin was the first to appreciate the potential of radial tire technology. He knew how to produce the new-fangled product and bring it to market. And he possessed the leadership qualities to convince a large corporation and industrial sector, both very much bound by tradition, to embrace his bold vision.

Michelin's view of work was inspired by his Christian faith. He saw work as a process of participating in God's act

---

12. J. Couretas, "Philosopher on the Factory Floor: The Sacramental Entrepreneurship of François Michelin." Acton Institute for the Study of Religion and Liberty, on-line commentary (www.acton.org), May 14, 2003.

of creation and saw nobility in the efforts of people to create the best possible products. He believed he was doing God's work in challenging his colleagues to new heights of creativity. As John Couretas has observed: "Michelin's is essentially a sacramental view of life in the sense that he everywhere sees the synergy, the cooperative exchange, between God and man."[13] This led him to the insight that propelled Group Michelin to world leadership: human creativity—not the calculations and projections of technocrats—is the wellspring of business success.

For François Michelin business is not first and foremost about making money. It is about serving the customer and people within the business. Of course, there are business people who "practice the capitalism of the jungle," says Michelin, "but one does not ban marriage because there are pederasts."[14]

The sciences also offer scope for grand visions. Take the case of Jérôme Lejeune, the French geneticist who, in 1958, identified the genetic defect that causes Down's Syndrome. This outstanding scientist in the 1970's became the moral leader of the pro-life movement in France and other European countries. Lejeune, one of the most highly regarded geneticists of the twentieth century, upheld the dignity of human life at a time when courts and tribunals and parliaments were usurping the divine right to determine who shall live and who must die.

For Lejeune, the legalization of abortion was not just morally objectionable; it constituted an assault against and an expression of contempt for science. Genetics demonstrated

---

13. Ibid.
14. F. Michelin, "The Heart of Mystery, The Heart of Enterprise." Acton Institute for the Study of Religion and Liberty, on-line commentary (www.acton.org), January–February 1999.

that at the very moment the ovum is fertilized by the sperm, all of the genetic information that defines the resulting individual is already inscribed in its entirety in the first cell. No new genetic information enters into an egg at any stage after its initial fertilization. Thus, genetic science postulates that a human being could not be a human being if not first conceived as a human being. Laws legalizing abortion rest on a theory of embryonic evolution—the embryo is not a human life but becomes one later on—with no basis in genetic science.

Jérôme Lejeune spoke the truth fearlessly and tirelessly: "If a law is so wrong-headed as to declare that 'the embryonic human being is not a human being', so that Her Majesty the Queen of England was just a chimpanzee during the first 14 days of her life, it is not a law at all. It is a manipulation of opinion, and has nothing to do with truth. One is not obliged to accept science. One could say: 'Well, we prefer to be ignorant, we refuse absolutely any novelty and any discovery.' It's a point of view. I should say, it's a 'politically correct' point of view in some countries, but it's an obscurantist point of view, and science abhors obscurantism."[15]

In view of the moral relativism and intellectual skepticism so prevalent in the European culture of his (and our) time, Lejeune's cause seemed doomed from the start. But, as his daughter Clara said of him, "his realism was inspired by a formidable hope."[16]

Religion, like science, also calls forth leaders possessed of magnanimous visions. One of the greatest religious visionaries of modern times was Josemaría Escrivá, the founder of

15. J. Lejeune, "Child, Family, State: Scientific Progress and Human Rights." Address to a conference of Bulevardi Foorumi, Helsinki, April 1990.
16. See C. Lejeune, *Life is a Blessing: A Biography of Jérôme Lejeune*. Ft. Collins, CO: Ignatius Press, 2000, p. 9.

the Roman Catholic organization Opus Dei.[17] Pope John Paul II called him "an apostle to the laity in modern times."[18]

Escrivá founded Opus Dei in 1928 at a time when holiness was considered the privilege of a select few—priests, monks, and other religious. He believed every Christian is called to sanctity. He insisted that Christian laymen would achieve sanctity through the faithful fulfillment of their daily professional, familial, religious, and social obligations, or not at all. He saw work not as punishment for Original Sin, but as a gift from God that sustains life and allows mere mortals to be co-creators of the world with God. Work well done is a vehicle for the worker's sanctification and a sacrifice to be offered to God for the salvation of souls. Although many "respectable" ecclesiastics considered Escrivá in his lifetime to be a heretic and a fool, multitudes heeded his call to sanctity the world over. An estimated 350,000 attended his canonization on October 6, 2002 in Saint Peter's Square.

John Paul II, another spiritual giant of the twentieth century, had a grand vision which could be summarized in the phrase from sacred scripture with which he inaugurated his long pontificate, "Be not afraid," and in those with which he ended it, from his personal Testament: "To humanity, which at times seems to be lost and dominated by the power of evil, egoism, and fear, the risen Lord offers as a gift his love that forgives, reconciles, and reopens the spirit of hope."

The Polish Pope began his pontificate at a time when the Catholic Church seemed more like a corpse than a living organism. Over a period of 25 years, he instilled a new pride in and loyalty to the Church among millions of Catholics,

---

17. See V. Messori, *Opus Dei: Leadership and Vision in Today's Catholic Church.* Washington, D.C.: Regnery Publishing, 1997.
18. John Paul II, *Rise, Let Us Be on Our Way.* London: Jonathan Cape, 2004, p. 117.

above all among youth. The hope of which he spoke was not sentimental but authentic and theological, a hope rooted in faith and calling forth heroic witness and heroic deeds.

The vast throngs of young men and women who greeted the Pope on his many journeys abroad and spontaneously gathered in St. Peter's Square to support him during his death agony bore witness to the powerful impact of his personality and message on mankind. When he died on April 2, 2005, the Catholic Church, whatever its problems, was vibrantly alive.

John Paul II was a Slav Pope whose philosophy of history took its inspiration not from Hegel and the rationalist philosophers, but rather from such great Polish and Russian thinkers as Adam Mickiewicz and Vladimir Soloviev. Far from excluding God from human history, he sought to identify the signs of the times requiring a concrete response from contemporary Christians. As the Pope's biographer George Weigel observed: "It was precisely because John Paul II is convinced that God is central to the human story that he could, by calling men and women to religious and moral conversion, give them tools of resistance that communism could not blunt."[19]

Lech Walesa attributes to Pope John Paul II the inspiration for the labor union Solidarity and its peaceful character: "He did not ask us to make a revolution, he did not ask for a *coup d'état*; rather, he suggested that we define ourselves. . . . Then the Polish nation and many others woke up."[20]

No less than politics, business, science and religion, literature is a privileged field for the exercise of magnanimity.

---

19. G. Weigel, *op. cit.*, p. 173.
20. L. Walesa, address to a joint session of the Polish parliament marking the 25th anniversary of the founding of the Solidarity labor union, August 2005.

Soon after he was arrested Aleksandr Solzhenitsyn understood the meaning and scope of his mission: to become the powerful and universal voice of the millions who had perished under communism. "I will publish everything! Tell all I knew! Touch off the explosive charge that had been piling up since I first saw the box cells of the Lubyanka, through all those winter work parades in the Steplag; for those who had been stifled, shot, starved, or frozen to death."[21] Solzhenitsyn understood he had to cry out the truth "until the calf breaks its neck butting the oak, or until the oak cracks and comes crashing down. An unlikely happening, but one in which I am very ready to believe."[22]

A writer who set to himself such an exalted goal—in such a time and in such a place—this was for the whole of humanity and for Russia in particular a sign of a formidable hope. The Russian poet Olga Sedakova, who read Solzhenitsyn in *samizdat*, witnesses:

"This new knowledge of the scope of the evil called forth by Communism, which could get a man killed if he were not prepared, hardly exhausted Solzhenitsyn's writings. By their very existence and narrative power, they said something more—namely, that even such an evil, although mightily armed, was not omnipotent! They gave us, quite obviously, a lease on life. This was more astounding than anything—one man versus virtually all of the regime's vast machinery of lies, stupidity, brutality, and ability to cover up evidence. This was a conflict waged by a solitary fighter such as comes along once in a millennium. And in every sentence, the victor's identity

_____

21. Aleksandr Solzhenitsyn, *The Oak and the Calf*. New York: Harper and Row, 1975, p. 292.
22. Ibid., p. 190.

came through unmistakably. But unlike the victories won by the regime, this one had nothing bombastic about it. I call it an Easter victory, one that passes through the medium of death to resurrection. In the *Archipelago* narrative, people rose from the dead, transformed in the dust of the camps, the country rose from the dead, the truth rose from the dead . . . It was the resurrection of truth in man and the truth about man out of the complete impossibility that this could happen . . ."[23]

A leader, to one degree or another, is a dreamer. Parents have dreams for their children, teachers have dreams for their students, managers have dreams for their employees, and politicians have dreams (as opposed to ideological fantasies) for their people.

Whether they lead many or few, leaders are always original, even though their dreams may involve traditional content. Leaders are adept at casting received wisdom in a new light, revealing its continued relevance to contemporary circumstances.

A leader's vision is never dull or boring. It illuminates the mind and the heart and lifts the spirit. It is something that can be *communicated* to others. Almost by definition, it must become a *shared* vision. An authentic leader is never in the position of being the only one who knows where the enterprise is headed, while the others follow blindly, like sheep. Yes, a leader has *followers*; but where trust and communication exist, these followers become happy collaborators, *partners* in a noble enterprise.

---

23. Olga Sedakova, "The Strength That Does Not Abandon Us." *Foma*, Moscow, December 2008.

THE SENSE OF MISSION

For the leader, a vision gives rise to a mission, which is then translated into action. Many people have dreams and visions, but leaders have the unique ability to concretize them as missions. To do this we need first of all to have a *sense of mission*, to be open to the very concept.

Everyone has a mission, or, if you will, a vocation, whether he or she knows it or not. A mission/vocation is not something we invent or imagine. It is a specific calling to do a certain thing and to be a certain way. It is what God expects of us. We need to discover what that is and correspond to it. Our mission/vocation will define our specific way of being, thinking, and acting all our days. It is the criterion by which we measure everything, and the principle that gives unity to the whole of our lives.

Small-minded men pass through life as through a tunnel, and with their "tunnel vision" see only themselves. "Men are born without teeth, without hair, and without ideals, and the majority of them die without teeth, without hair, and without ideals," said Alexandre Dumas. But great men are open to possibilities beyond the limitations of the self, and are restless until they have said "yes" to their vocation.

A leader's sense of mission/vocation mirrors his conception of marriage and family life. Small-minded men see family life as a *means* to essentially selfish ends—to eat well and get the laundry done, or to stave off loneliness, or gain in social respectability, or the like. Great men, by contrast, understand family life to be a vocation to sacrifice all for the sake of others.

A family is a unit of love and communion destined to grow. If it is not that, it is at risk. A family is not a collection of sovereign individuals who share the same refrigerator, as

21

some sociologists would have us believe. Nor is the home a pit stop between trips to the office.

Leaders see family as a mission. Some even feel the necessity to write down a family mission statement reflecting common values and giving direction to family members.

The mission of parents is to raise their children towards responsible adulthood. No objective is more important than this. Being constantly aware of this mysterious and sacred mission turns parents into authentic leaders—into men and women of greatness.

Leaders cultivate a sense of mission in professional life. They conceive of work as a vocation, as an opportunity to serve, and thus grow in maturity and personal greatness. How different from those who see work in purely utilitarian terms—as a means of self-affirmation, or of escaping a domestic situation they find unsatisfactory, or of accumulating wealth, or the like. They are likely to be functionaries rather than leaders. They may get the job done, but they invariably fail to blaze a trail. The structures they leave behind are makeshift—here today, gone tomorrow. The authentic leader, by contrast, builds for the ages. He leaves behind cathedrals.

Missions improve people and society and strengthen group identity. To be effective, they must embrace positive human values and be well articulated. Many organizational mission statements deal in generalities and have little bearing on employees' day-to-day activities. This is a lost opportunity. The corporate mission must affect each employee's performance on a day-to-day basis: it must become integral to the functioning of the organization from top to bottom.

As Steven Covey has noted: "An organizational mission statement—one that truly reflects the deep shared vision and values of everyone within that organization—creates a great unity and tremendous commitment. It creates in people's hearts and minds a frame of reference, a set of criteria or guidelines, by which they will govern themselves. They don't need someone else directing, controlling, criticizing, or taking cheap shots. They have bought into the changeless core of what the organization is about."[24]

A vigorous sense of mission can sometimes fall victim to the tyranny of financial objectives and mundane business realities. When this happens, Management by Objectives (MBO) tends to take over, and mission ceases to serve as a decision-making criterion. The problem with MBO is that it focuses management's attention on what the company wishes to achieve, rather than on *why*. If you do not know *why*, it will be very difficult to say exactly *how*, and you will have a hard time winning people's wholehearted commitment.

Management by Mission (MBM) is the way to go. MBM helps restore the primacy of mission throughout the organization by taking an integral approach to performance evaluation. Employees are evaluated for their contribution to the enterprise's mission, as well as the achievement of financial and operational goals. Thus, the focus on results is maintained, but with a view to the long-term realization of the organization's values.

Organizational behavior specialist Pablo Cardona puts it this way: "The most important benefit of MBM is that by making missions a part of the management system, the organization helps managers to be true leaders; in other words, it helps them to inspire a sense of mission in their subordinates."[25]

---

24. S. Covey, *op. cit.*, p. 143.

25. P. Cardona and C. Rey, "Management by Missions: How to Make the Mission a Part of Management." Occasional Paper, IESE Business School, Barcelona, March 2003 (revised February 2004).

MAGNANIMOUS MEANS TO MAGNANIMOUS ENDS

Magnanimity comprises not only the mission, but also the *means* by which to carry it out.

Leaders make their dreams come true through hard work and persistence, qualities that distinguish magnanimity from vanity: "Vanity," says the French philosopher Reginald Garrigou-Lagrange, "loves the honor and prestige that comes from great things, whereas magnanimity loves the work and effort that has to be done to achieve them."[26]

Leaders are in close touch with everything that makes up reality, the little things as well as the big. "Great souls pay much attention to little things," says Escrivá, "for many 'littles' can amount to an enormous sum."[27] "Have you seen how that imposing building was built? One brick upon another. Thousands. But one by one. And bags of cement, one by one. And blocks of stone, each of them insignificant compared with the massive whole. And beams of steel. And men working, the same hours, day after day. . . . Have you seen how that imposing building was built? By dint of little things!"[28]

Leaders choose material means proportionate to their mission and their practical objectives. They are not stingy or tight-fisted. They possess the mentality of entrepreneurs: first they set the objectives; then they acquire the means to meet their objectives. They avoid the pitfall of first acquiring the means and *then* fashioning an objective from them, a not uncommon practice labeled "effectuation" in the business literature.

---

26. R. Garrigou-Lagrange, *The Three Ages of the Interior Life*. Rockford, IL: Tan Books and Publishers, 1989, p. 84.
27. See J. Escrivá, *The Way*, nos. 818 and 827. New York: Scepter Publishers, 2002.
28. Ibid., no. 823.

CHALLENGING PEOPLE TO LEAD

The leader is always striving to grow, to improve, and is deeply concerned that those around him do the same. He or she has no nobler responsibility than seeing to the personal and professional improvement of others.

The *sine qua non* of improvement is the emotionally mature and intelligent desire to overcome oneself and to help others do likewise. This desire stems from a deep awareness of the exalted vocation of man. "Leadership," says Drucker, "is the lifting of a man's vision to higher sights, the raising of a man's performance to a higher standard, the building of a man's personality beyond its normal limitations."[29] This challenge applies both to the leader, and, through the leader, to the led. Leadership indeed is never an individualistic exercise. True leaders are always *leaders of leaders*.

For leaders, the achievement of high organizational goals is never an end in itself, but only a means to the higher end of growth for all concerned.

In 1951, Escrivá urged a few of his followers to set up a university in the Spanish city of Pamplona—the future University of Navarre. The objective was demanding, but within a comparatively short period of time, the university had built up prestigious faculties of medicine, journalism, architecture, and other disciplines and would be considered perhaps the finest private university in Spain. Its graduate business school—IESE—would establish campuses in Barcelona and Madrid and be ranked one of the world's leading providers of executive education.

When the university was still in its start-up phase, Escrivá met with the dean of the medical school and asked him why he had come to Pamplona to work.

---

29. P. Drucker, *op. cit.*, p. 157.

"To help set up the university," he replied.

Escrivá's swift and energetic response: "My son, you went to Pamplona to become a saint; if you achieve this goal, you will have achieved everything."[30]

To establish a university is indeed a great thing; but to learn, to grow, and to serve others while accomplishing a great mission is what makes a man great.

Leaders challenge people to grow. They are not satisfied with colleagues who do not make waves. They always demand of them the utmost in effort. They want nothing more than that they achieve their full potential as professionals and as people. "If we treat people as they are," says Goethe, "we make them worse. If we treat them as they should be, we guide them to where they should be."

Magnanimity is always prudent, patient, and realistic. If you set exorbitantly high standards, you could discourage employees and might even harm them. Leaders should not set their people up for a fall, nor should they drive or coerce them. Such behavior is imprudent and unjust. It retards personal progress in trying to compel it.

CONCLUSION

Magnanimity implies prudence, but not the false prudence that reflexively advises caution in the face of great undertakings. In this regard, Garrigou-Lagrange says: "This prudence, which has as its principle: 'Undertake nothing,' is that of cowardly souls. After saying: 'The best is *sometimes* the enemy of the good,' it ends by declaring: 'The best is *often*

---

30. A. Vázquez de Prada, *The Founder of Opus Dei*. New York: Scepter Publishers, 2005, vol. 3, chapt. 20.

the enemy of the good.'"[31] False prudence ("let's not overdo it") is mediocrity masquerading as virtue.

Sadly, some people take a dim view of magnanimity. At the end of the 1990s, a group of friends and I launched *Russian Solidarity*, a program aimed at helping disadvantaged people in Russia, mainly in and around Moscow and Saint Petersburg. Annually, some thirty students from the United States and various European countries work together renovating the living quarters of poor, elderly people, renovating churches destroyed by the Communists, and the like.

The students raise money to cover the expenses of their stay in Russia. They work hard, resting only on weekends to do things like play soccer with inmates of Russian juvenile prisons. We designed *Russian Solidarity* not to solve this or that social problem, but to foster magnanimity in young people. Thus, as we help poor people materially, we are also helping our students to get outside of themselves. They learn about working in teams, about friendship, about the joy of self-giving, about the high importance of social solidarity. *Russian Solidarity* is a program focused on the welfare of both the recipient and the giver.

The reaction of the local population has been extremely positive. They are grateful for and amazed by the generosity of the foreign students. But a few people—mainly intellectuals—have reacted negatively.

They say it would be better that the funds raised to support the project be spent by an NGO doing philanthropic work or given directly to poor people. Perhaps so, but then it would be a different program with very different objectives. *Russian Solidarity*'s critics cannot grasp the value of giving

---

31. R. Garrigou-Lagrange, *op. cit.*, p. 84.

young people the opportunity to grow in generosity, to instill in them an appreciation for the value of personal sacrifice for the sake of others.

Magnanimity is not madness. "Magnanimity," wrote Escrivá, "means greatness of spirit, a largeness of heart wherein many can find refuge. Magnanimity gives us the energy to break out of ourselves and be prepared to undertake generous tasks, which will be of benefit to all. . . . The magnanimous person devotes all his strength, unstintingly, to what is worthwhile. As a result he is capable of giving himself. He is not content with merely giving; he gives his very self."[32]

---

32. J. Escrivá, *Friends of God*, no. 80. New York: Scepter Publishers, 2002.

CHAPTER 2

Humility

The Ambition to Serve

> Whoever would be great among you must be
> your servant.
>
> —*MATTHEW 20:26*

THE LEADER'S MAGNANIMOUS VISION is directed to the service of others—his family members, clients and colleagues, his country, and the whole of humanity. This noble ambition to serve is one of the fruits of the beautiful virtue of humility.

As humility is often misconstrued, let us take a moment to clarify its meaning.

"Humility," says the German philosopher Josef Pieper, "is not primarily an attitude that pertains to the relationship of man to man: it is the attitude of man before the face of God."[1] Indeed, humility is a *religious* virtue. It impels man to acknowledge his status as a creature of God. The thought that God is everything and he is nothing does not upset him.

---

1. J. Pieper, *On Hope*, chapt. 2 in *Faith. Hope. Love.* Ft. Collins, CO: Ignatius Press, 1986, p. 99.

On the contrary, he finds ennobling the notion that God has willed him into being.

The ancient Greeks extolled the virtue of magnanimity, but they failed to grasp the true meaning of humility, because they lacked the concept of *creatio ex nihilo*—creation out of nothing. The mystery of *creatio ex nihilo* is a gift of the Judeo-Christian tradition, although it can be inferred by natural powers of reason.

Humility thus is an attitude that pertains to man's relationship to God; it is *the habit of living in the truth*—the truth about one's metaphysical situation and about one's virtues and defects.

Humility is also an attitude that pertains to man's relationship to man. Thanks to humility, leaders spontaneously reverence what is of God in every creature. This reverence fosters the ambition to serve. Leaders serve God present in others. In doing so consistently, they develop *the habit of service*.

In contrast to humility, pride engenders not truth but falsehood, not service but selfishness. If I fail to grasp the essential truths about myself and other people, I will begin to lose touch with reality. Pride will transform my interior self into a fictitious realm; it will blind me to the beauty of service.

People afflicted with such existential blindness are in need of what the Greeks called *metanoia*—a true conversion of the heart. *Metanoia*, which literally means "beyond the mind," pushes you beyond the limits of your usual thoughts and feelings, imparting a complete change of perspective, a reformulation of life goals—a change of life as such. Modern psychology calls this process a "paradigm shift" or "breakthrough." But these concepts do not begin to reflect the magnitude of the transformation required to overcome the existential alienation generated by pride.

HUMILITY AND MAGNANIMITY

Magnanimity (the striving of the spirit towards great things) and humility (abasement before God and what is of God in others) go hand-in-hand and cannot be rent asunder. While He was on earth, Jesus Christ did not need to strive for things great by ordinary human standards, but he accomplished no less a feat than man's divinization and eternal happiness. By the same token, He did not need to abase Himself before God and what is of God in others, yet, as it turned out, this was precisely part of the achieving of his grand vision for humanity: He took the form of a servant,[2] died on the Cross, and offered His body to humanity as spiritual food.

Unfortunately, *humility* has acquired a pejorative connotation. The humble person often is seen as devoid of ambition and nobility and unworthy of honor.

Many Christians propagate a false understanding of humility by their behavior. Some are too prone to submit meekly to "fate" or to the judgment of the wicked; they fail to understand that profound reverence *for what is of God in others* is not the same thing as abject abasement before authority. Some lack the boldness to strive for perfection in personal and professional life; they ignore Christ's injunction to "be perfect, as your heavenly Father is perfect."[3] Some pretend that it is better to sin "humbly" than to strive for perfection "proudly," as if sinful behavior had nothing to do with pride and self-improvement nothing to do with humility.

This false humility is the refuge of the small-minded. It is not virtue. It is self-castration, and it crudely contradicts human dignity. This is the sort of humility Nietzsche had in

---

2. See Phil 2:5–7.
3. Mt 5:48.

mind when he branded Christian morality a morality fit for slaves.

People who are falsely humble give short shrift to God, society, and, not least, themselves. They fail to live up to their obligations and shirk responsibility: "That false humility is laziness," writes Escrivá. "Such a 'humility' leads you to give up rights that are really duties."[4]

The humble man sees himself as he really is. He acknowledges his weaknesses and shortcomings, but also his strengths and abilities. "To despise the gifts that God has given is not due to humility, but to ingratitude," writes Thomas Aquinas.[5]

The word humility comes from *humus*, which is essential to the fertility of soil. Humility is indeed fertility, not sterility.

"Humility and high-mindedness," says Pieper, "not only are not mutually exclusive, but actually are neighbors and akin. . . . A 'humility' too weak and too narrow to be able to bear the inner tension of cohabitation with high-mindedness is not true humility."[6]

Thanks to the tension between humility and magnanimity, leaders avoid the pitfall of taking themselves too seriously. Their awareness of the gap between the grandeur of their vision (magnanimity) and their own inability to bring it about (humility) makes them laugh at themselves with simplicity and good humor. The small-minded laugh at themselves only ironically, the proud not at all.

Humility starts out as a seed lodged deep in the heart. It develops through an exercise of the will, and finally blossoms when leaders implement the three great principles

---

4. J. Escrivá, *The Way*, no. 603.

5. Thomas Aquinas, *Summa Theologiae*, II, q.35, a.2 ad 3.

6. J. Pieper, *Fortitude and Temperance*. New York: Pantheon Books, 1954, pp. 99–100.

of managing people in organizations: *inclusion*, *collegiality*, and *continuity*.

INCLUSION: HUMILITY IN GOVERNANCE

Leaders set high standards of performance, which they expect others to follow. They achieve this result not through browbeating but encouragement. This is inclusion. It means that *leaders pull rather than push, teach rather than command, inspire rather than berate*. Thus, *leadership is less about displays of power than the empowerment of others.*

Leaders solicit, acknowledge, and make use of the contributions of all members of the organization in solving problems. But inclusion has little to do with democracy: "Having a say differs from having a vote," says Max De Pree, former CEO and writer on management.[7] Inclusion can always be practiced, even in very hierarchical organizations.

Leaders do not interfere in the tasks of subordinates without good reason. They trust their capacity to do the job.

President Thomas Jefferson once offered this retort to Pierre S. Du Pont de Nemours, the founder of the industrial giant that still bears his name: "We both consider the people as our children, and love them with parental affection. But you love them as infants whom you are afraid to trust without nurses."[8]

Leaders assume their colleagues are free, mature, and responsible human beings—not children. They are happy to see them develop a sense of their own worth by contributing to the common purpose of the organization.

---

7. M. De Pree, *Leadership is an Art*. New York: Dell Trade Paperback, 1990, p. 25.
8. See J. O' Toole, *Leading Change: The Argument for Values-Based Leadership*. New York: Ballantine Books, 1995, p. 32.

Leaders do not do the work of subordinates for them. They are happy to advise and to encourage, but otherwise the co-worker must resolve the matter to the best of his abilities. Inclusion is not paternalism, which is ineffective because those on the receiving end learn nothing and only wind up losing their self-respect. Parents who tidy up the rooms of their adolescent children are a clear example of ineffective paternalism.

Leaders delegate power, which means they transfer decision-making to a subordinate and make him co-responsible for the results. When properly done, delegation confers on the employee in question a wonderful opportunity to learn, to grow professionally, and to rise in the esteem of colleagues.

The leader trusts the employee to whom he has delegated authority. He remains interested in the matter at hand but tries to remain detached from it so that the employee can take possession of it. He is at the employee's disposal if he needs help and makes sure the employee knows this, but otherwise refrains from interfering.

Leaders assume full responsibility for the results—both good and ill—of delegating authority to others. This requires humility. The proud manager delegates authority to a subordinate, then blames him when things go wrong. This practice only impedes the decision-making skills of the employee, for he will now have every incentive to pass the buck back to the boss when faced with difficult decisions.[9] In short, true delegation is a balanced relationship of co-responsibility. False delegation is a farce in which no one is quite certain "who's on first."

---

9. See P. Ferreiro and M. Alcázar, *Gobierno de Personas en la Empresa*, PAD, Escuela de Dirección, Universidad de Piura, 2002, chapt. 9.

"Inclusion," says Bennis, "makes people feel that they are at the heart of things, not at the periphery. It makes them feel and act 'as if they own the place' in the words of Max De Pree. It gives them a sense of human bond, a sense of community, and a sense of meaning in their work. Inclusion or involvement means that the leader believes in and acts on the inherent dignity of those he leads."[10]

When inclusion prevails, many lead, others aspire to lead, and everyone in the organization understands that leadership will be rewarded. The more inclusion becomes ingrained in the culture, the more centers of leadership will proliferate. The net result is the strengthening of the organization as a whole.

Inclusion is the reverse of a "command-and-control" approach, which, in the last analysis, is a manifestation of pride. The proud manager believes he is the indispensable man. He rarely solicits employees' contributions, is loathe to delegate, and intervenes, quite unnecessarily, in the work of subordinates. This pride-based model of interaction is not only ineffective, it seriously damages the organization: creative people leave, the mediocre stay, and trust, enthusiasm, and initiative wither on the vine.

It has been said that the practice of inclusion is difficult for men and easy for women. It is certainly true that men are, by temperament, more inclined than women to "go it alone" and to rely on aggression to achieve their goals. But leadership is about humility, which is a virtue of character developed by practice. It is not a trait of temperament to be found in greater supply in one sex or the other. Virtue is an equal opportunity phenomenon.

---

10. W. Bennis and J. Goldsmith, *op. cit.*, p. 5 and p. 8.

COLLEGIALITY: HUMILITY IN DECISION-MAKING

Collegiality means decisions are not made by the leader alone but by the leader together with all of the organization's other decision-makers. It is the virtue of prudence in action: five people working together see farther and more deeply than one person working alone. But collegiality is above all a demonstration of the humility of the leader who is aware of his own limitations and desires to serve his colleagues by developing in each of them a sense of freedom and a sense of personal responsibility: everyone participates in making decisions, and everyone responds to them.

The leader is a servant of his team, as a collective, and of each one of its members, as individuals. He does everything in his power to deepen the commitment of team members to their shared mission.

In team meetings, he encourages colleagues to voice (even critical) opinions, to cut short pointless digressions, to see the positive side of every proposal, to come up with solutions rather than waste time bemoaning problems, and always to question received, majority opinion. The leader, of course, practices what he preaches in leading his team to prudent decisions for the common good of the organization. In doing so, he has another objective: to help each team member improve professionally and personally. Thus, he draws out members who are reticent, curtails the loquacious, encourages domineering types to give way now and then, and helps pessimists to see the positive side.[11]

In building a team culture in this way, the leader succeeds in getting colleagues to see that more benefits flow when people work together than when it's "every man for himself."

---

11. See "Leadership in Work Teams," a technical note by Profs. P. Cardona and P. Miller, IESE Business School, Barcelona, January 2000.

The leader willingly renounces his judgments (unless principles are at stake) when the group decides against his position. In the event things subsequently go awry, he does not say, "This wouldn't have happened if you had listened to me." He participates enthusiastically in the implementation of all decisions and shares personal responsibility for them with colleagues.

Collegiality has a dual benefit—it develops decision-makers and protects the organization from egregious misrule or what one might call dictatorship.

Dictatorship stems from pride. The proud manager thinks (erroneously) that he is master of all he surveys. He overestimates his professional and moral capabilities and underestimates those of others. He is hard to deal with because he tends to be mistrustful and overly sensitive. One-man-rule is inefficient and ineffective: co-workers learn nothing of the art of governance and fail to develop a sense of freedom and responsibility.

One-man-rule may be adopted when there is consensus on its necessity (in situations of extreme hardship, for example), but then only briefly, since extended periods of autocracy can hinder the formation of mature decision-makers.

Collegiality is a moral principle valid in business, social, and political organizations equally. Here is Philippine President Cory Aquino on collegiality in politics: "The ability to work well with others, to listen to different points of view, to credit such views with a sincerity equal to one's own, and to have the flexibility to accommodate the valid concerns of others: this is an important quality for anyone who wishes to serve the people. It is an expression of the spirit of service. Indeed, how can anyone claim to have a genuine spirit of solidarity with the people in general, if he is incapable of an operational solidarity with those he must work with closely?"[12]

---

12. C. Aquino, *op. cit.*

THE PRINCIPLE OF CONTINUITY

Continuity tends to be assured when leaders promote their organizations, rather than themselves. Leaders come and go, but the organization remains. They have achieved success if they have created and/or developed strong organizations that thrive long after they have left the scene.

A proud boss, by contrast, tries to convince others that things were bad under the *ancien régime* and his predecessor was not up to the job. He may also attempt to impose unnecessary stylistic changes around the office, all in an effort to demonstrate to colleagues that they are living in a new era—*his* era.

Leaders do not make themselves irreplaceable. They share information. They create the conditions for others to bring their work to a successful conclusion.

One of a leader's most vital functions is to choose his closest collaborators and pave the way for succession. As Max De Pree points out: "Leaders are responsible for future leadership. They need to identify, develop, and nurture future leaders."[13]

Some leaders seem determined to set the firm up for failure after they leave, the better to burnish their own reputations for success at the expense of their hapless successors. The CEO succession at Rubbermaid is a case in point. During the tenure of CEO Stanley Gault, Rubbermaid routinely appeared in *Fortune*'s list of "America's Most Admired Companies." His leadership methods were effective but, by his own admission, tyrannical. In the end, the succession was bungled and the firm began a long downward trajectory. His successor lasted a year on the job and had to contend with an ineffective management team. Gault had done little to foster the kind of talent at the top that would

---

13. M. De Pree, *op. cit.*, p. 14.

lead the firm into the future. As Jim Collins observes: "Gault did not leave behind a company that would be great without *him*. . . . Gault's successors found themselves struggling not only with a management void, but also with strategic voids that would eventually bring the company to its knees."[14]

ALTRUISTIC MOTIVES

The desire to serve springs from the virtue of humility, which, in turn, springs from the same sources as all of the other virtues—the heart, the will, and the intellect. But humility, more than any other virtue, is rooted in the depths of human personality. One serves, first and foremost, because one values being of service. This indicates something about one's motives in the realm of action.

Human motives are various. They include making money (material motivation), acquiring useful knowledge and skills (professional), developing one's character (spiritual), serving others (altruistic), and/or glorifying God (religious). Typically, a person engages in professional work with more than one of these motives, and sometimes for all of them. In fact, motives are interrelated. A desire to earn money (material motivation) is more likely to be fulfilled if one increases one's knowledge and skills (professional motivation). Similarly, those who wish to serve others (altruistic motivation) typically seek to develop their characters by practicing the human virtues (spiritual motivation) and by giving glory to God (religious motivation).

Religion, indeed, especially Christian religion, gives the most radical and convincing answer to the question, "Why must I serve others?" Christians do so because they see Jesus

---

14. J. Collins, *op. cit.*, pp. 26–27.

Christ in each and every human being. They serve humanity for God's sake.

Can we love and serve humanity without reference to God? The great Russian writer Fyodor Dostoevsky answered this question 150 years ago: "You cannot replace the absence of God with love for humanity, because people will ask immediately, 'Why do I have to love humanity?'"[15]

I may serve others for a while out of sentimentality, fellowship, or to prove (if only to myself) that I am a good person. But when difficulties arise and heroism is called for, I may well conclude that the price is too high for what I get in return.

The religious motive is the one best suited to instill in us a desire to serve unconditionally, despite all vicissitudes, to the end of our days. This is so because this motive allows us to see God in other people.

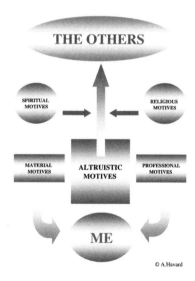

15. In "*Mysli, vyskazyvania i aforizmy Dostoevskovo.*" Paris: Pyat' Kontinentov, 1975, p. 107.

There are those who imbue their work with a religious spirit. Their main concern is to please God by serving others. Such people work in *conspectu Domini*—in the presence of God. They could not care less if anyone notices their good deeds. The thought of earthly recognition simply does not enter their minds.

I remember an episode that well illustrates this phenomenon. I was once invited to address a conference on educational reform in Saint Petersburg, Russia. Although it was a frigid morning, I had considered not wearing my winter coat because the lining had been badly torn when it got caught in a revolving door the previous day. But it was cold, so I wore it anyway.

I arrived at the conference hall, handed my coat to an elderly lady at the coat-check counter, and ascended the grand staircase to the conference room.

When the event ended, the same elderly lady brought me my coat. I thanked her, went on to dinner, and eventually arrived back at my hotel. Removing my coat, I was astonished to notice that its lining had been exquisitely repaired.

It was the work of the elderly lady at the coat-check counter. She was not the employee of a major corporation with a mission statement talking about the firm's "dedication to uncompromising personalized service," but rather of a state enterprise that had no interest in service of any kind and paid paltry wages.

The beauty of her work moved *me*. So did her selflessness, her concern for me (a complete stranger), and her desire to . . . *pass unnoticed*. She received nothing for what she did, no extra money, no recognition, and no thanks from me because she did not tell me what she had done. She did what she did—as Russians would say—*before the face of God*.

A person with altruistic motives stops working the moment he has met the other persons' needs through the available means. A person with only professional motives neglects his work the moment he starts getting bored or when he thinks there is nothing left to learn. A person with only material motives makes the minimum effort to obtain the maximum salary.

People with only material or professional motives need external control. People with altruistic motives do not.

When determining whom to *promote*, the leader must take into account not only an employee's productivity and efficiency, but also his *motivation*, especially if the promotion is from a technical job to one involving supervising people. The employee whose motivation is to serve others is a better fit for such a position than one whose motives are mainly financial, no matter how admirable his professional abilities. It would be better to give such an employee a raise, but leave him in his current position until he changes his attitude.

Promotion must not be the only way to make more money. The corporate graveyard is littered with the corpses of firms that failed to see the link between promotion and motivation. We must not give an employee power over other people if he lacks altruistic motives. He would destroy the organization.

A CORPORATE CULTURE OF SERVICE

Mature human beings seek not only a decent salary and interesting things to do, but also the means to develop themselves as persons, to serve others, to find a sense of meaning in their work. They will happily cast their lot with those who, in a spirit of service, help them to meet their material, professional, spiritual, and religious needs. This is how loyalty develops.

Loyalty cannot be bought. People are loyal to leaders when leaders are loyal to them. When Enrique Shaw (1921–1962), the Argentinean businessman and founder of the Christian Association of Corporate Leaders, was dying of cancer, 260 workers came to the hospital to give blood for a life-sustaining transfusion.

Polls show decreasing employee loyalty to management, because management's loyalty to them is increasingly dubious. A nationwide survey of U.S. employees, conducted by Aon Consulting in 2001, found that only 45 percent would remain in their current job if offered a similar job elsewhere with slightly higher pay.[16]

The leader who would reinforce the altruistic motives of those around him must himself embody such motives. In doing so, leaders lay the foundation for the development of an organizational culture that is both attractive and effective. The loyalty of management to employees is reciprocated and is soon felt by clients, whose loyalty to the firm increases. Clients respond with friendship and trust and recommend the firm to others, thereby becoming the firm's valued partners. Thus, a corporate culture of loyalty and trust leads to high rates of client retention—one of the keys to business success.

Here managers of firms must be aware of the crucial difference between "serving in order to gain" and "gaining in order to serve."

Serving in order to gain implies the predominance of material motives. You serve only as long as you gain, then you stop. Clients usually suspect your true motive.

16. See P. Koestenbaum, *Leadership, The Inner Side of Greatness*. New York: Jossey-Bass, 2002, p. 54.

Gaining in order to serve implies the predominance of altruistic motives. You serve the client to meet his needs until the job is brought to a fully satisfactory conclusion. The gain will come afterwards, as a reward not directly sought, as payment for excellence in service. For a client to prefer doing business with you and not your competition, it is not enough for you to like your job, be a great professional, and offer a superior product. Clients reward you for your altruistic motives, your concern for their real needs.[17]

When students ask me for an example from my own professional experience of my having gone the extra mile to provide my clients with world-class service, I often think of an episode that occurred when I was working as a lawyer and a young couple engaged my services in handling their divorce. (I am not a divorce lawyer; in Europe, where I practiced law, the legal profession is less specialized than in the United States.) I listened closely as they told me their tale of woe—all about how they were completely incompatible, no longer loved one another, and had concluded that the only thing to do was to put an end to their union of nearly three years.

They now wanted my advice on how to decouple their lives in the easiest, most painless manner possible. They asked me what I thought. I said, "I think you're a couple of idiots." It was evident to me—although I had never laid eyes on them before—that these were sincere and decent souls who had entered a period of turbulence in their lives. Instinct and experience of life told me it was a storm that would soon pass. I urged them not to throw in the towel, to give the situation time, and not do anything rash. For several days, I heard nothing from them. I wondered how they were getting

---

17. P. Ferreiro and M. Alcázar, *op. cit.*, chapt. 3.

on. Finally after about 10 days, they called me. They said they had decided to remain together and thanked me profusely.

This episode occurred fifteen years ago. They are still married and have several children. And they remain clients of the law firm! Clearly this is not your typical case study in how to retain clients by providing breakthrough service, at least not one a major business school would publish. But it contains a relevant lesson for anyone in professional life. We humanize the world of work when we engage with the people around us—clients and colleagues—in deep kinds of ways. We cannot be cool or indifferent to the people who cross our path. We have a moral imperative to give of ourselves. The consequences will only be positive—friendship will grow, the atmosphere in the work place will be transformed, our ability to attract clients and retain them will increase dramatically. It is simply a matter of striving to maximize the happiness of clients and employees and close collaborators.

An attitude of service fosters a rich and genuine corporate culture marked by trust in management, commitment to the company's mission, and cooperation among all employees.

A corporate culture of service accomplishes the following:

- *Generates excellence in customer service:* Employees "gain in order to serve," rather than "serve in order to gain." Customers are the beneficiaries and remain loyal over time.

- *Promotes change:* A culture of service increases the ability to adapt to major, even radical, change in the economic, political, and social environment by fostering individual initiative, knowledge-sharing and organizational learning.

- *Enhances prospects for survival:* Companies marked by a high level of trust and commitment have an easier time surviving a fall in profit margins, thereby improving their chances of surviving crises.

- *Earns higher profits:* A lower level of trust and commitment entails high control costs, a poor flow of information within the firm, and a lack of identification with the strategy designed by top management. Studies show that in the medium and long terms, firms that enjoy high levels of trust and commitment are more profitable than those that do not.[18]

CONCLUSION

Management guru Jim Collins spent five years researching the leadership qualities of executives who raised the level of their companies' performance from good to great. He found that humility on the part of leadership is vital to making the great leap forward, and identified two types of leader when it comes to this indispensable virtue:

The first has no intention of subjugating his ego to the needs of the common good. In Collins' words: "For these people, work will always be first and foremost about what they *get*—fame, fortune, adulation, power, whatever—not what they *build*, create, and contribute."[19]

The second type sees the role of leader as an opportunity to serve others and achieve the common good. Those who hold this view are often people who received strong human formation from loving parents, friends, and mentors. Not a few are religious or have undergone a religious conversion or similar life-altering experience.

---

18. See J. Pfeffer, *The Human Equation*. Cambridge: Harvard Business School Press, 1998.
19. J. Collins, *op. cit.*, pp. 36–38.

Just Say No

> You will never say yes, unless you learn to say no.
>
> —*ALEKSANDR ZORIN, CONTEMPORARY RUSSIAN POET*

THE NOBLE VIRTUES of magnanimity and humility are losing ground to the rampant egoism of modern culture, manifested in current philosophical trends, modes of behavior, and social conventions. The first step towards becoming a leader is to be aware of this state of affairs. The next is to declare your independence from it.

Get used to saying no.

Say no to egoism. Modern philosophy, which began with René Descartes and culminated in Emmanuel Kant, created a new system of thought that broke with the tradition of the ancient Greeks. They replaced Greek *realism* with a new way of thinking called *immanentism*. Realism means that I can grasp the reality—the *res*, the thing, the object—that exists outside my mind. Immanentism, on the contrary, means that what I perceive is not an objective reality, but a possibly delusional product of my mind and conscience.

Immanentism leads to *existential indifferentism*. If I am unable to grasp objective reality, I will never explore, wonder, or contemplate. Nothing will speak to me and I will respond to nothing. My heart will never take flight. It will grow cold to meaning and mission and vocation.

If we cannot grasp objective reality or objective truth, we will soon be in thrall to techniques and systems, production and consumption, pleasure and entertainment. And leadership? Leadership will become a game of strategies and tactics, empty rhetoric, and techniques for manipulating people.

Before Kant, man sought to discover his place in the cosmos; after Kant, man tries to produce the cosmos in his mind. Some call this autonomy; I call it terminal egoism.

Say no to cynicism. Niccolò Machiavelli's *The Prince*, a practical handbook of the political arts written with a view to helping Florence's ruling Medici family consolidate and expand its power, cynically extols the role of deception and manipulation in politics. For Machiavelli, virtue and power do not mix. Indeed virtue can undermine the prince's hold on power, whereas vice tends to promote it. The prince, therefore, should use all expedient means to accomplish his end, including deceit.

Machiavelli continues to inspire value-free forms of leadership to this day. There are plenty of leadership seminars on the market that teach methods for manipulating employees psychologically. These owe a lot to Machiavelli. A book with the suggestive title *Machiavelli for Managers* was published not too long ago.[1]

The reality is that if my ends and means fly in the face of human nature and dignity, I will only lead people astray.

---

1. E. and L. Spagnol, *Machiavelli per i manager*. Milano: Longanesi, 1988.

Consider the careers of Lenin, Hitler, and Mao, who killed millions of innocent people in the name of ideology. Consider also Margaret Sanger, who in the name of eugenics initiated a process that has killed hundreds of millions of unborn children.* These world figures are far from being examples of genuine leadership; indeed, only deeply confused people would see leadership in prevaricators and mass-murderers. To understand the kinds of forces that inspired such individuals, a reading of Machiavelli's *The Prince* is useless; *The Demons* by Fyodor Dostoevsky would be more to the point.

I find dismaying lists of the greatest leaders of the twentieth century published by major news magazines that lump authentic heroes like Reagan, Walesa, and John Paul II together with such evil despots as Lenin, Hitler, and Mao. Juxtapositions of this sort are deeply misleading. They only confuse the public by morally equating purveyors of hope with falsifiers of hope.

Say no to materialism. Management specialist Chester Barnard once observed: "I have found it impossible to go far in the study of organizations without being confronted with a few questions which can be simply stated. For example: 'What is an individual? What do we mean by a person?' The temptation is to avoid such difficult questions, leaving them

---

* Margaret Sanger (1879–1966)—tireless zealot on behalf of contraception, compulsory sterilization, and abortion. The founder of Planned Parenthood, the largest abortion provider in the United States, she advocated compulsory sterilization to discourage "unsuitable" people from having children so as to perfect the human race. In 1919, Sanger wrote in the magazine she founded, *Birth Control Review*, "More children from the fit, less from the unfit—that is the chief issue of birth control." Although not as famous as Hitler and Lenin, Sanger had an enormous impact on our civilization. In 1931, H.G. Wells, who considered her the "greatest woman in the world," wrote: "When the history of our civilization is written, it will be a biological history, and Margaret Sanger will be its heroine." (See D. de Marco and B. Wiker, *Architects of the Culture of Death*. Ft. Collins, CO: Ignatius Press, 1988.)

to the philosophers and scientists who have been debating for centuries. It quickly becomes apparent, however, that . . . we cannot evade them entirely. . . . All sorts of people, especially leaders and executives, act on the basis of fundamental assumptions or attitudes regarding the answers to these questions, although they are not usually aware of the fact."[2]

I cannot serve people if I see them as cogs in a machine, devoid of spirituality and transcendent value. My treatment of people, even if pleasant in outward expression, will sooner or later become unpleasant in substance. The word "humanism" on my lips, even if pronounced with passionate grandiloquence, will sound as false and cynical as the word "comrade" in the old Soviet Union.

Say no to technocratic management. Leadership is not a technique. It does not focus on systems and structures, but on people. It is not about *know how*, but about *know what* and *know why*. It is not about "doing things right," but about "doing the right things."**

Leaders certainly need to possess technical skills, but these are not nearly enough. "Managers who only understand methodology and quantification," says De Pree, "are modern-day eunuchs. They can never engender competence or confidence."[3]

Unfortunately, modern civilization produces more technicians of management, law, medicine, and science, than real managers, lawyers, doctors, or scientists. The people it produces will have a hard time finding a job in the near future,

---

2. C. I. Barnard (1886–1961), *The Functions of the Executive*, 1938, quoted by Juan Antonio Pérez López in *Teoría de la acción humana en las organizaciones*, Madrid: Rialp, 1991, pp. 17–18.

** In the words of P. Drucker, "Management is doing things right; leadership is doing the right things."

3. M. De Pree, *op. cit.*, p. 55 and p. 71.

because "people who think and behave like machines," says Peter Koestenbaum, "will be replaced by machines. Every job that can be automated will be automated. The only non-automated jobs left will be leadership jobs. There will be no more work for those who do not make the leadership choice. This dilemma will be a key problem facing humanity in the third millennium."[4]

Say no to radical individualism. The individualist is there only to serve his own interests. He does not want to be influenced by anyone and has no desire to influence anyone else. The leader, by contrast, wants to influence others and be influenced by them. He aims to receive spiritual benefits from others and to enter into the lives of those around him so as to exercise a positive influence.

Human beings absorb influences, good, bad, and indifferent, as sponges do water—from parents, teachers, friends, the media, etc. People are social beings by nature. They live in communities and are therefore never free in an absolute sense. "If it were possible to conceive of a human being in a state of absolute freedom," wrote the Russian film director Andrei Tarkovsky, "he would resemble a fish out of water. . . ."[5]

Human freedom is not liberation from external influences, which is impossible in any case. Rather, it is a question of *freely* choosing the influences you *freely* choose to submit to. One who chooses wisely has a chance of becoming a magnificent human being.

Leaders understand this perfectly well. At various points in their lives they have freely chosen to submit to the

---

4. P. Koestenbaum, *op. cit.*, p. 37 and p. 39.
5. See A. Tarkovsky, *Sculpting in Time*. Austin: University of Texas Press, 1989, chapter "On the Responsibility of the Artist."

beneficent influence of loving parents, a prudent friend, a magnanimous teacher, or any combination of the same. The danger comes when we submit, consciously or unconsciously, to negative influences. If my human formation comes mainly from Hollywood, I will scarcely understand what positive influence is until I begin to notice its absence in my own life.

Say no to "group-think." The Orwellian concept of "group-think" (an early phrase for political correctness) stems from the Enlightenment Project of the eighteenth-century French *philosophes*. They tended to view human beings mechanistically as cogs in the social machine. Having no concept of intrinsic evil, they attributed social problems to dysfunctional human behavior, which could be eradicated through social engineering carried out by enlightened "initiates." The Enlightenment, in T.S Eliot's phrase, is about "dreaming of systems so perfect that no one will need to be good."[6] The Enlightenment denied what humanity had known since the dawn of time: that evil is intrinsic to man—and good as well.

The Enlightenment has produced much negative fall-out, not least a tendency to make people indifferent to developing virtue in themselves and those around them. Why bother when social engineering will take care of everything? In the Enlightenment view, what counts is not man and his character, but the interests of "progressive humanity."

"The most serious problem within modern liberal societies," writes Nicholas Capaldi, "is the presence of the failed or *incomplete* individual. . . . What really inhibits these people is . . . a character defect, a *moral inadequacy*. Having little or no sense of individuality, they are incapable of loving what is

---

6. T. S. Eliot, *The Rock*. New York: Harcourt Brace, 1934.

best in themselves; unable to love themselves, they are incapable of loving others; incapable of loving others, they cannot sustain life within the family; in fact they find family life stultifying. What they substitute for love of self, others, and family is loyalty to a mythical community. . . . What they end up with are leaders who are their mirror image: leaders who are themselves incomplete individuals and who seek to control others because they cannot control themselves."[7]

The incomplete individual substitutes political slogans and psychobabble for virtues. Tolerance, understood as moral relativism, replaces the virtue of justice, statistics and probability theory replace prudence, avoidance of nicotine and trans fats and other dietary fads replaces self-control, self-esteem replaces magnanimity, self-criticism replaces humility—and democracy replaces God.

The result is pervasive *boredom*—"not simply boredom of the day-in, day-out, quotidian sort but boredom on a transcendent, even metaphysical plane: a kind of boredom with the mystery of life itself."[8] A boredom that "renders the imagination inert and desire torpid."[9]

---

7. N. Capaldi, "Distributive Justice or Social Justice," in D. Anderson, ed., *Decadence: The Passing of Personal Virtue and its Replacement by Political and Psychological Slogans*. London: Social Affairs Unit, 2005, p. 145.

8. G. Weigel, *op. cit.*, p. 166.

9. D. B. Hart, "Religion in America: Ancient & Modern," *The New Criterion*, March 2004, vol. 22, p. 6. Cited in G. Weigel, *op. cit.*, p. 167.

PART II

PRACTICAL WISDOM
AND WILL POWER

To the leadership-specific virtues of magnanimity and humility, we add four attributes of character known traditionally as the cardinal virtues—prudence, courage, self-control, and justice.

Prudence enhances our ability to make the right choices, *courage* to stay the course and resist pressures, *self-control* to subordinate our emotions and passions to the spirit, and *justice* to give every person his due.

If magnanimity and humility are the essence of leadership, the cardinal virtues constitute its foundation.

CHAPTER 1

Prudence
Making the Right Decision

> The pre-eminence of prudence means that so-called "good intention" and so-called "meaning well" by no means suffice.
>
> *—JOSEF PIEPER*

THOSE WHO WOULD LEAD people and serve them and the common good need to develop the capacity to make right decisions. They need to cultivate prudence, the virtue that makes us effective decision-makers.

Prudence enables leaders to perceive situations in all their complexity (or simplicity, as the case may be) and make decisions in accordance with this perception.

Prudent decision-making consists of three steps: deliberation (gathering information so as to establish a yardstick), judgment (the evaluation of that information), and deciding. The deliberative aspect is directed towards reality, whereas the judicatory aspect and the ultimate decision have to do with will and action.

THE KNOWLEDGE GRANTED BY PRUDENCE

In order to make right decisions, leaders need to possess the professional knowledge appropriate to their field of activity. No less important is knowledge of human beings.

Leaders need to be students of human nature. They must possess philosophical and moral knowledge about people, derived from academic study and life. This knowledge will help them deal effectively with professional situations that are more human than technical in nature.

Even *this* is not enough, however. Decision-makers must cultivate the virtue of prudence, otherwise known as practical wisdom. For example: before deciding to undertake a particular initiative, the CEO will need to know if the organization has people capable of implementing it. This kind of knowledge is granted by prudence, not by academic study or technical acumen.

Although decision-making is more effective when imbued with prudence, prudence is no guarantee of success. There will always be risks and uncertainties in the implementation phase. Our CEO, however prudent he may be, cannot be scientifically certain that the people available to him are capable of implementing his decision. "The prudent man," says Pieper, "does not expect certainty where it cannot exist, nor on the other hand does he deceive himself by false certainties."[1]

Scientific decision-making is most likely to succeed when the matter at hand is of a purely technical nature. In leadership, such cases are rare because human beings are invariably involved. Scientific decision-making is an illusion, although that doesn't prevent politicians and planners, victims of their rationalist education, from devising formu-

---

1. J. Pieper, *Prudence.* New York: Pantheon Books, 1959, p. 37.

las to guarantee the success of their policies and decisions. Their inclination towards "scientific" decision-making limits their personal effectiveness while undermining the confidence of their colleagues.

Shakespeare's Hamlet is a good example of how an obsessive desire for certainty can result in imprudent decision-making. Hamlet craves information to give him greater certainty, but in the end he fails to act. Shakespeare's masterpiece is indeed a "tragedy of indecisiveness."

We do not develop the virtue of prudence through life experience, but through contemplation of that experience. We must learn to use it to grow in spiritual acuity and develop the knack for perceiving reality as it really is. In this way, we enhance our powers of diagnosis and intuition.

Thus, decisions based on personal experience *alone* will tend to be directed towards the past, not the future. Indeed, situations we face now are never carbon copies of the past. They are always new and unique. Experience has value; but it is the combination of experience with contemplation that makes for effective, prudent decision-making.

DELIBERATION

Prudent decision-making consists of three steps, sometimes taken consciously, sometimes not: deliberation, judgment, and decision.

Deliberation is reflection so as to grasp the contours of the situation at hand. Here are some pointers.

First, gather information and analyze it critically. This means assessing the reliability of sources and distinguishing between facts and opinions, truths and half-truths.

Aleksandr Solzhenitsyn relates a dramatic example of a half-truth in *The Gulag Archipelag*o, his searing account of the Soviet concentration camp system. He reports his amazement at coming across an article in a Soviet nature magazine on the discovery in the Siberian tundra of the fossilized remains of prehistoric fish and salamander. They were found encased in a subterranean ice lens, actually a frozen stream, which had preserved them in a state of perfect freshness for tens of thousands of years. The magazine further reports that those who unearthed these amazing specimens bolted them down . . . *with relish* . . . on the spot.

Contrary to the reporter's intention, the article's interest for Solzhenitsyn and the source of his amazement lay not in the scientific discovery, but in the members of the excavating party. The journalist neglected to report their identity, but Solzhenitsyn understood immediately. Their behavior gave them away. They were denizens of a hidden world never described or alluded to in the media, never accorded public recognition of any kind, because its existence was a state secret—the world of the Gulag Archipelago. Solzhenitsyn understood that only Gulag inmates dying of hunger could have bolted down prehistoric salamanders with relish on the spot.

Soviet readers like Solzhenitsyn were accustomed to reading between the lines. But what of readers in democratic societies where people are accustomed to taking things at face value?

Confusing fact and fiction has become commonplace in our society. Many are not so well educated as to be immune to the false messages propagated by the media. We must take care to sift the information and messages we receive, screening them through a filter. This does not mean suspecting manipulation in everything; but we do need foster a healthy critical spirit in ourselves and in others.

It is important always to remember that, according to Oliver Thompson, "the most dangerous propaganda is the kind which is not recognized as such, either by its audience or even by its perpetrators. It is the steady 'drip, drip' of aggressive, prejudiced, or materialistic ideas which those competing to be social leaders project through all the media in their fight for personal success."[2]

Avoid rationalizations at all costs. To rationalize is to twist objective data, consciously or unconsciously, to make them fit pre-conceived notions. Rationalization is a psychological process that distorts reality until it accords with our passions and interests. Thus, instead of seeking solutions to our problems, we are prone to seek problems that fit our solutions.

A typical example of rationalization is the case of a manager who raises his voice to employees on the theory that they will perform better if they're afraid of him. Other examples are expressed in platitudes such as, "The customer is always right," "Everything is relative," "Every opinion is equally valid," "The majority is always right," "All's fair in love and war." We may find such untruths comforting, but if we act on them, we will have a hard time practicing the virtue of prudence.

It takes courage to live by truth and avoid rationalization. At times the tyranny of fashion and politically correct attitudes leads us almost automatically to reject certain truths because we find them hard to accept.

Once I gave a lecture on European law to a group of teachers steeped in the spirit of secular materialism. I was

---

2. O. Thompson, *Mass Persuasion in History: A Historical Analysis on the Development of Propaganda Techniques.* Edinburgh: Paul Harris Publishing, 1977, p. 132. Cited in D. Anderson, ed., *Decadence, op. cit.*, p. 106.

explaining the principle of subsidiarity, which holds that the supreme, central authority (Brussels) should perform only those tasks that cannot be performed effectively by lesser jurisdictions (EU member states). When I explained that this constitutional principle was derived from Roman Catholic social doctrine, the assembled teachers broke out laughing. They said I was crazy. I had an uprising on my hands. They could not and would not accept facts that did not fit their (secularist) vision of the world. I could have cited passages from Pope Leo XIII's encyclical *Rerum Novarum* of 1891 and Pope Pius XI's *Quadragesimo Anno* of 1931, both written well before the establishment of the European Union and both stating and defining the principle of subsidiarity, but the assembled teachers would not have listened to me. They were fit to be tied, and like the scribes and Pharisees who stoned Saint Stephen to death, they "stopped their ears and ground their teeth against me."

Recognize and put aside your prejudices. Rationalization has its roots in cowardice. Prejudice stems from ignorance.

To overcome our prejudices we need to practice humility. "One of the characteristics of authentic leaders," writes Covey, "is their humility, evident in their ability to take off their glasses and examine the lens objectively. . . . Where there are discrepancies (prejudice, ignorance, or error), they make adjustments to realign with greater wisdom."[3]

Once I was strolling through a park in Helsinki in my long winter coat, lost in thought. A ten-year-old Finnish girl came up and asked: "Are you a spy?" I smiled and assured her I was not. She was visibly relieved. She had a prejudice, a preconceived notion of spy derived from hearsay or from movies: tall man, long coat, deserted city park, autumn leaves—all of

---

3. S. Covey, *Principle-Centered Leadership*. New York: Simon & Schuster, 1992, p. 20.

that meant spy. She was wrong. Her prejudice had led her astray. Nevertheless, she was a leader in the making, because she had the humility to put her intuition to the test.

Some years later, I had a similar experience in Warsaw. I was strolling through the streets of a quiet residential district in my long winter coat, when I was apprehended by members of the Israeli secret service on suspicion of being a terrorist (hardly!) and given the third degree by three formidable, armed men. Their error was rooted in a preconceived notion: I was sauntering in the vicinity of the embassy, did not look like a local Varsovian, and was wearing that long winter coat.

There's more to the story of my vexed winter coat. Recently in Moscow I was going to a Christmas liturgy at the invitation of a friend of mine—a Russian Orthodox priest. The service was taking place on the uppermost floor of a tall building. I was entering the elevator in my notorious coat when a man wearing a yarmulke got on right behind me. He looked me over with interest and asked: "Are you a Jew?" I said no. All the time we were in the elevator, he continued staring at me, perplexed. Finally he said: "It's dishonorable to conceal your ethnic identity." Something about the coat convinced him I was Jewish.

We all have our prejudices. Some choose to believe that a man in a long winter coat is engaged in espionage, others that he is hatching a nefarious plot, still others that he is a co-religionist when he isn't one. Much depends on our upbringing. But by practicing humility, leaders, in Covey's words, "make adjustments to realign with greater wisdom."

Keep in mind the nature of your organization. If you are head of a primary school or director of a charitable institution, it would be imprudent to tackle problems in the manner of a corporate business leader. Certainly, you need to be a good manager, but you are not "in business" and should always keep that in mind. Otherwise, you run the risk of making decisions that harm your organization.

Once in Estonia I directed a leadership seminar for a group of school principals. It was shortly after the fall of Communism, and everybody was trying to get into business. Even schools were under pressure to adopt commercial methods and criteria. When I explained that a grade school and a commercial enterprise were two different things, Kersti Nigesen, a principal whom I had known since Soviet times and respected for her "tough love" approach to the profession, said with emotion, "Alexander, you probably do not understand the importance of what you're saying. My people and I really needed to hear that! A few months ago a speaker told us that our school had no future, because we still hadn't switched to running it like a business!" Her school—the Vanalinna Hariduskolleegium— was and remains Estonia's leading public school. The main reason for its success is that management refuses to run it as a business.

Keep in mind your organization's mission. Specific objectives should advance the organization's mission or, at a minimum, not contradict it. The mission should drive and give meaning to the objectives, not the other way around. Successful accomplishment of the mission must be management's foremost decision-making criterion.

A mission without objectives is an exercise in futility. Similarly, the achievement of objectives unlinked to any overarching mission is much ado about nothing. If your goal is to become number one in a particular industry, you must ask yourself "why?" A company's mission is the contribution it makes to the common good, not its ability to outdo the competition.

Try to foresee as many consequences of your actions as you possibly can. The Latin word *prudentia* stems from *providentia*, which means foresight. Prudence is thus both "insight" (a vision of reality as it is before you act) and "foresight" (a vision of reality as it will be after you have acted).

Sometimes we go through life blind, unable to foresee the consequences of our actions. We have all experienced situations in which we lacked the most basic foresight, with results that are sometimes funny, sometimes tragic, and sometimes a combination of both. To wit:

My friend Tobias, whom I had not seen for fifteen years, paid me a visit in Finland. It was February and I wanted him to experience the delights of the Nordic winter. Along with some friends, we rented a small house for the weekend on an island in the archipelago of the Gulf of Finland. The temperature was below zero, and the sea was frozen over with the exception of a channel cut by a ferryboat, which sailed every hour between the island and the mainland.

One evening, we partook of the traditional Finnish sauna. After half an hour of intense heat, Tobias and I decided to walk across the ice and jump into the channel to cool down. But we hadn't foreseen the problem of how to get out of the water and back onto the ice. There was no ladder and the edge of the ice was slippery. After several unsuccessful attempts to exit the frigid waters, we were seized by the realization that, absent a miracle, we would be dead within minutes.

We at least had the consolation that a deep night, a frigid wind, a half moon, and a million stars would accompany us during our last moments of earthly existence. Tobias and I were paying a steep price for our imprudence. But then I noticed that the freezing wind beating on my wet skin had caused my arms to stick to the ice. This gave me leverage to haul my legs up on to the ice and to safety. I then reached down and pulled Tobias out of the water. We lived to tell the tale.

In attempting to foresee the likely consequences of our actions, it helps if we can draw on relevant personal experience. But if we lack such experience, as I did, we need to have recourse to the experience of others. For example, when Finns go skiing on frozen lakes, they take awls with them, so that if the ice breaks under them they can drive the awl into the ice and haul themselves to safety. Of course, Finns do not take awls or knives to the sauna, but then they are not so stupid as to throw themselves into icy waters that offer no way out.

Apply natural moral law to specific situations so as to assure a just outcome. It is not enough to know the Ten Commandments and draw the proper conclusions. Prudence—practical wisdom—is called for. From "Thou shalt not bear false witness," we may derive the corollary, "Thou shalt not slander thy competitor." Fine, but we must prudently determine for ourselves the limits of fair competition. From the Decalogue's prohibition against stealing comes the corollary, "Thou shalt pay a just wage." OK, but what is a just wage in any given case? We must make this prudential judgment. Leaders face a plethora of daunting moral and ethical challenges whose solutions are rarely to be found in reference books. There is no hard-and-fast "technique" of excellence; excellence requires an infinite capacity for adaptation, which comes from the virtue of prudence.

Finally, *seek advice.* The prudent person is not a know-it-all but one who makes right decisions. Leaders recognize their limitations and choose associates who can challenge them.

The founding fathers of the United States, says James O'Toole, "did not hire yes-men. George Washington's greatest strength was the supreme self-confidence that allowed him to assemble—and heed the advice of—a team of men who were each far more brilliant than the president they loyally served. . . . But even the few presidents so competent as to make it impossible to find people more capable than themselves—Jefferson, Lincoln, and Theodore Roosevelt—went out of their way to assemble brilliant cabinets and staffs."[4]

Leaders do not hire as close collaborators people who determine which way the wind is blowing and adjust accordingly. On the contrary, they seek collaborators who will face problems with courage, ingenuity, and determination.

It is usually not enough to seek out sound, objective, disinterested advice. Sometimes you need the advice of people who know you well and care about you.

"A friend," says Pieper, "and a *prudent* friend, can help to shape a friend's decision. He does so by virtue of that love which makes the friend's problem his own, the friend's ego his own (so that after all it is not entirely 'from outside'). For by virtue of that oneness which love can establish he is able to visualize the concrete situation calling for decision, visualize it from, as it were, the actual center of responsibility."[5]

Leaders feel free to accept or reject the advice they receive. They make *personal* decisions and take *personal* responsibility for them. If things go wrong, they do not blame others for having given them bad advice.

Deliberation is the first step in prudent decision-making. Shakespeare's Othello meets a cruel fate brought on by his

4. J. O' Toole, *op. cit.*, p. 30.
5. J. Pieper, *op. cit.*, p. 55.

failure to deliberate. Ever impulsive, he jumps straight to the conclusion without stopping to think. He shoots first and asks questions later.

JUDGMENT AND DECISION

Deliberation is followed by judgment and decision. To judge is to weigh pros and cons. To decide is to choose between alternative solutions.

Decision-makers should take the time—assuming they have this luxury—to gather all relevant information and analyze all of the factors that could influence their decision. But once the course of action is clear, they must act quickly.

André Philip, the French Socialist Deputy, wrote about Robert Schuman, the Father of Europe: "By temperament Schuman was timid. . . . He often delayed decisions. . . . But as soon as he was sure of what his interior voice demanded of him, he suddenly made the most daring decisions and carried them out no matter the consequences; he was then impervious to criticism, attacks, and threats."[6]

Prudence is not only *insight* and *foresight*. It is also *imperium* or command. It directs the implementation of decisions expeditiously and with authority.

Prudence is not timorous; leaders run great risks in making decisions. "Nobody," says Drucker, "learns except by making mistakes. The better a man is the more mistakes will he make—for the more new things he will try. I would never promote a man into a top-level job who has not made mistakes, and big ones at that. Otherwise he is sure to be mediocre. Worse still, not having made mistakes he

---

6. See R. Lejeune, *op. cit.*, Prologue 2.

will not have learned how to spot them early and how to correct them."[7]

If arrived at prudently, a mistaken decision is not necessarily a wrong decision, just as a decision that turns out well is not right if it was imprudently made. A prudent decision may turn out to have been a mistake and an imprudent one a success because new factors came into play during implementation that could not be foreseen during the deliberation phase.

It is advisable, therefore, not to judge a leader's capacity for prudential judgment on the basis of the results of just *some* of his decisions. Rather, it should be judged on the totality of the results achieved under his stewardship.

Leaders carry out their decisions no matter how hard the going may get. If a decision provokes a counter-reaction, this is not necessarily a sign that the decision was wrong. On the contrary, it may be a sign that the decision was good and opportune.

When Teresa of Avila began a reform of the Carmelite order in 1562, few people, whether clerical or lay, wished to be reminded of how God wanted them to live. Carmelites who rejected her reforms started a campaign against her. Other orders joined in, the civil authorities initiated legal proceedings against her, and some of her enemies threatened to haul her before the Inquisition. She often had to enter a town secretly in the middle of the night to avoid causing a riot.

John of the Cross, co-founder with Teresa of the Discalced Carmelites, suffered similar trials.

Many Carmelite friars resisted his reforms. He was imprisoned for more than nine months in a small, stifling cell, and punished in a manner usually reserved for hardened criminals.

---

7. P. Drucker, *op. cit.*, p. 145.

In the face of extreme persecution, Teresa and John proceeded calmly. The violent counter-reaction did not stop them. They knew they had to restore the Church to health and this would require surgery. They knew it would be painful for everybody. But their perseverance brought remarkable results: in relatively short order, their reforms swept Spain and all of Europe.

BEING AND PERCEPTION

At the heart of the virtue of prudence is the relationship of a leader's character to his ability to grasp reality. In other words, the relationship between being and perception, between *what we are* and *what we see*.

Our ability to perceive reality and make proper judgments depends on the degree to which we live the classical virtues. As Aristotle put it, "the good man judges each class of things rightly, and in each the truth appears to him."[8] The proud man, on the contrary, judges as true whatever flatters his pride; the intemperate man, whatever may grant him power, money, or pleasure; the small-minded man, whatever justifies his cowardice or laziness.

The relationship between being (understood as strength of character) and perception (understood as insight into the essence of things) is profound. We perceive and interpret things through the lens of character. By strengthening our character—i.e., by growing in virtue—we improve our ability to deliberate in the light of reason.

Our character tends to determine what we make of people—and we are always sizing them up. We often project our defects onto others. If we crave power, we are likely to

---

8. Aristotle, *Nicomachean Ethics*, 3, 4.

believe that those around us do the same, whether or not this is true—and usually it isn't.

Saint Augustine suggests a way to avoid false judgments about the character and motivations of others: "Try to acquire the virtues you believe lacking in others. Then you will no longer see their defects, for you will no longer have them yourself."[9]

If we possess virtues in abundance, we will have an easier time seeing people as they really are, with all their strengths and weaknesses.

Virtues enlighten our intellect, strengthen our will, and purify our feelings. They enable us to perceive the world, human situations, and people as they really are, and not as we imagine them to be. Without this objectivity, we cannot make right decisions.

Objectivity does not mean impartiality. Leaders make objective decisions that are to some degree subjective. *Prudent decision-making does allow for preferences. In the same situation different leaders, all equally prudent, may arrive at different decisions.*

---

9. St. Augustine, *Enarrationes in psalmos*, 30, 2, 7 (PL 36, 243).

CHAPTER 2

Courage
Staying the Course

> Staying the course, maintaining a consistent focus,
> and being predictable in terms of what we believe
> may not always lead to love, but will lead toward
> effective leadership through trust.
>
> —*WARREN BENNIS*

AS WE HAVE JUST SEEN, prudence is vital to effective decision-making. But courage also plays a vital role. Courage helps leaders avoid rationalizations, overcome their fear of mistakes, enact decisions with dispatch, and persevere when the going gets tough.

Yet courage has ramifications that far transcend decision-making.

A DEFINITION OF COURAGE

Let's start by saying what courage is not. It is not fearlessness. The best and bravest of soldiers experience fear before going into battle. Jesus Christ was so terrified of his impending torture and execution that he sweated blood. Fearlessness often stems from an inability to size up reality correctly—a potentially dangerous state of affairs. Fearlessness can also arise from an asceticism that suppresses human passions—among them fear. To suppress fear is to suppress courage.

Courage is the sacrifice of self for the realization of prudent and just goals. The link between sacrifice of self and nobility of purpose is vital. After all, a terrorist can sacrifice himself, but that does not make him courageous; in fact, he is a malicious lunatic. You can lay down your life for a fanatical cause, but this is not courage. It is the result of obstinacy, pride, delusional thinking, and in some cases, the spirit of evil.

If my values are skewed, I will not be courageous, although I may be tough. And if I value sacrifice for its own sake, I may be stoical, but stoical does not mean courageous.

"Neither difficulty nor effort causes virtue," writes Pieper, "but the good alone. Fortitude therefore points to something prior. . . . Prudence and justice precede fortitude. . . . Only he who is just and prudent can also be brave."[1]

In order to be courageous, it is not enough to act according to one's conscience. Many terrorists act according to their conscience. Courage begins when I educate my conscience through a sincere and systematic search for truth.

ENDURANCE

When we think of courage, we think of boldness and daring, and rightly so. But courage can also be monotonously humdrum; it often calls for endurance over time.

Endurance is the essence of courage. Endurance is not passivity, for it requires a strong, proactive spirit. In endurance man's inmost and deepest strength reveals itself. It

---

1. J. Pieper, *Fortitude and Temperance.* New York: Pantheon Books, 1954, pp. 18–19.

can be harder and entail greater courage for a soldier to be pinned down in a cold, damp foxhole than to charge into a hale of bullets with all flags flying.

Endurance means that leaders maintain the integrity of their conscience, even in times of trial.

In fidelity to his conscience Sir Thomas More, the great humanist and Lord Chancellor of King Henry VIII, refused to take an oath recognizing Henry as self-proclaimed head of a new English church of his own invention. For that reason More suffered martyrdom by decapitation. Although treated cruelly during his fifteen-month incarceration in the Tower of London, and despite the opposition of his king, the bishops of England, most of his friends, and his entire family (including, most painfully, his beloved daughter Margaret), Sir Thomas stood fast in his convictions.

Eleven terrorist attempts on his life failed to deter Russian Prime Minister Pyotr Stolypin from his efforts to reform the Russian peasantry. He remained true to his conscience, his mission, and his people.

Hours after a terrorist bomb exploded during a reception at his home killing 27 people and injuring 32, including two of his children, Stolypin, though barely recovered from the blast, repaired to his study to work on his reform proposal far into the night. With Russia on the brink of catastrophe, he understood that his duty as head of government was to drive through a sweeping reform of Russian life.

For Stolypin, the good of the nation outweighed his personal sorrow: in the terrorist attack, his fourteen-year-old daughter Natasha was left disabled for life. He knew that the only way to keep himself and his family out of harm's way was to resign his office, but he had no intention of acquiescing to terror. He wrote in his testament, "Bury me where I will be killed."

In daily life, leaders are consistent and precise in their conduct. They do not act immorally and then justify it by pointing to the general immorality around them (the notorious "everybody does it" argument). When they arrive at the office, they do not discard their values, as Escrivá used to say, "like a man leaving his hat at the door."[2]

Leaders are impervious to fashionable trends. The young Ronald Reagan was remarkably indifferent to which way the political winds were blowing. In the late 1940s and early 1950s, when Communists where fighting for control of Hollywood and most people in the film industry were turning left for reasons of career advancement, Reagan remained clear and candid about what he believed and why.

A lifelong Democrat, Reagan chose to become a Republican at the time least politically advantageous for himself. At the time, a popular Democrat, John F. Kennedy, was in the White House, and the Democrats controlled both Houses of Congress, while Republicans had been effectively out of power since the Great Depression and seemed inured to permanent minority status. Liberal orthodoxy was everywhere triumphant. But Reagan's motives were *not* first and foremost motives of self-interest. In the words of his White House speech writer, Peggy Noonan: "His lifelong struggle in whatever context he found himself was to determine what was right and then stand for it no matter what."[3]

Aleksandr Solzhenitsyn also bore unflinching witness to truth, and did so under a totalitarian regime sworn to his destruction. The nation's foremost writer, he suffered imprisonment and forced exile from his homeland.

Solzhenitsyn's reputation was high at home and abroad as long as he limited himself to criticizing Stalin, as in such

---

2. See J. Escrivá, *The Way*, no. 353.
3. P. Noonan, *op. cit.*, p. 66.

early works as *One Day in the Life of Ivan Denisovich*. This suited the purposes of the Soviet leader Khrushchev, who was conducting a campaign against Stalin's personality cult. It also suited many Western intellectuals, who admired the October Revolution but felt that Stalin had betrayed it.

In subsequent works, Solzhenitsyn made it clear that he opposed not only Stalin, but Lenin and the October Revolution. He even rejected the *February* Revolution. And he did not hesitate to write an open letter to the Soviet leadership setting forth his heterodox views. Thus, he earned the undying enmity not only of the Soviet regime, but also of the legions of Western intellectuals—many his erstwhile supporters— who were broadly sympathetic to the revolutionary cause and its secularizing aims.

Once disgorged into Western exile, he faced incomprehension and derision for his failure to pay obeisance to secular materialism. His growing army of detractors, unable to allow the legitimacy of a worldview that contradicted their own, soon made him out to be an enemy of all freedom and progress. Solzhenitsyn remained utterly unfazed.

In the course of the past thirty years, the abortion controversy has given the world numerous courageous leaders who patiently and with remarkable powers of endurance refused to submit to the trend of the times.

Jérôme Lejeune was a paragon of courage in the battle for life. With his discovery in 1958 of the cause of Down's Syndrome, he became world-famous and was touted as a possible recipient of the Nobel Prize. His discovery held out hope for a cure of the dread disease and opened up entirely new paths in the field of genetics. From the podium of a United Nations conference on health, he observed, "Life is a fact and not a desire." Appalled by the U.N.'s growing adherence to an ideological agenda opposed to life, he boldly

Pyotr Stolypin (1862–1911)
Russian Prime Minister under the last
Tsar (1906–1911). His sweeping reform
program combined justice for the dis-
possessed with a vigorous defense of
Russian traditions. He succumbed to
an assassin's bullet after having survived
eleven previous attempts on his life.
© *Foundation Stolypin*

Robert Schuman (1886–1963)
French prime minister and parliamentar-
ian during the Fourth Republic. His vision
of Franco-German solidarity after World
War II paved the way for the European
Union, earning him the title "Father of
Europe." © *Maison de Robert Schuman-
Conseil Général de la Moselle*

**Karl Franz Josef von
Habsburg-Lothringen
(1887–1922)**
The last Emperor of Austria-
Hungary (1916–1922). He was
the leading European head
of state to seek to end the
carnage of the First World War.
His devotion to peace and
justice was the hallmark of
his reign. © *Photo-postcard:
Arthur Brenda, d'Ora, Vienna
(Gebetsliga Archiv, Kaiser Karl-
Gebetsliga für den Völkerfrieden,
Sankt Pölten, Austria)*

Josemaría Escrivá (1902–1975)
Spanish priest and founder of Opus Dei. He taught that Christian lay people achieve sanctity in and through professional work and family life, or not at all. His writings emphasize the importance of the natural and supernatural virtues in ordinary life. © *Fundacion Studium, Madrid*

Ronald Reagan (1911–2004)
President of the United States (1981–1989). Known for his powers of persuasion, he worked to end the division of the world into hostile ideological camps, and restored American self-confidence after Vietnam and Watergate. *Courtesy Ronald Reagan Library*

Aleksandr Solzhenitsyn (1918–2008)
Russian novelist and Nobel laureate in literature (1970). His devotion to truth rooted in a Christian vision of man and society shook an officially atheist regime to its foundations. His name is a byword for moral courage in modern times. © *Corbis*

Above:
John Paul II (1920–2005)
Polish-born Roman Pontiff
(1978–2005). He steadied the
barque of Peter in turbulent
times, tirelessly preached
the Gospel in journeys to 117
countries, and bore public
witness to the redemptive
value of suffering.
Private collection

Left:
François Michelin (1926–)
Industrialist and chairman of
Group Michelin (1955–1999),
one of the world's leading
producers of tires. He believed
the main aim of business is
not profits, but serving clients,
employees and society at large.
© *Michelin*

Jérôme Lejeune (1926–1994)
France's leading geneticist, he identified the genetic cause of Down's Syndrome. He was also one of the moral leaders of the pro-life movement in the 1970s in France and other European countries.
Given by the Lejeune Foundation,

Cory Aquino (1933–2009)
President of the Philippines (1986–92). She mobilized "people power" to overthrow dictator Ferdinand Marcos and thoroughly transform the Philippines.
Private collection

Lech Walesa (1943–)
Gdansk shipyard electrician, founder of the Solidarity labor movement and President of Poland (1990–95). His insistence on justice for Polish workers provoked sweeping change in Poland and throughout Central and Eastern Europe. *Private collection*

challenged the international gathering: "Here we see an institute of health turning itself into an institute of death." Having spoken the truth without compromise, he confided to his Danish wife: "This afternoon I lost my Nobel Prize."

By insisting on upholding scientific truth and the larger moral truth that flowed from it, Lejeune flew in the face of the spirit of the times, the revolutionary spirit of May 1968. The atmosphere in which he found himself quickly became toxic. His daughter Clara recalls cycling past her father's university on her way to school. The walls were smeared with huge black letters: "Tremble, Lejeune! The Revolutionary Student Movement is watching!" and "Lejeune is a murderer. Kill Lejeune!" and "Lejeune and his little monsters [ed., children with Down's Syndrome] must die!" At meetings he was assaulted verbally, and sometimes physically. He no longer received invitations to international conferences on genetics. Funding for his research was cancelled. He was forced to disband his laboratory and research team.

Thus, a man who at 38 became France's youngest professor of medicine and held France's first chair in fundamental genetics, a man who had a splendid future ahead of him full of honors, recognition, and power, found himself in the prime of life with no collaborators, no funding, not even office space. He was dropped by his friends, excoriated by the press, and made into a social pariah. He accepted this state of affairs with all serenity and with the joy of having given no quarter to evil. He died on Easter Sunday, 1994, after a brief but agonizing illness that began on Wednesday of Holy Week.[4]

Mother Teresa of Calcutta, one of the greatest religious leaders of the twentieth century, also stood courageously

---

4. See C. Lejeune, *op. cit.*, p. 47, p. 54, and p. 110.

against the trend of the times. In her Nobel Prize lecture in 1979, she linked her defense of the unborn to the cause of peace: "I feel the greatest destroyer of peace today is abortion, because it is a direct war, a direct killing—a direct murder by the mother herself. Because if a mother can kill her own child, what prevents me from killing you and you from killing me?"

President Ronald Reagan fearlessly spoke out against abortion, although his aides warned him that it would hurt him in the opinion polls. No politician of the twentieth century spoke so forthrightly about the right to life. His famous speech of March 8, 1984, in which he famously denounced the Soviet Union as the "Evil Empire," dealt more with abortion and the soul of America than with Communism: "Human life legislation ending this tragedy will some day pass the Congress, and you and I must never rest until it does. Unless and until it can be proven that the unborn child is not a living person, then its right to life, liberty, and the pursuit of happiness must be protected. You may remember that when abortion-on-demand began, many warned that the practice would lead to a decline in respect for all human life, and the philosophical premises used to justify abortion-on-demand would ultimately be used to justify other attacks on the sacredness of human life, including infanticide or mercy killing. Tragically enough, these warnings are proving all too true."

Leaders refuse to become discouraged when the public rejects them and their ideas even to the point of vilification. Ronald Reagan was called an over-the-hill movie star, an affable dunce, and a warmonger. Josemaría Escrivá was called a heretic, a Communist, and a Fascist, and the organization he founded a mafia-like sect. Robert Schuman was denounced by many of his countrymen for holding out an olive branch to France's traditional enemy. His opponents accused John Paul II of indirectly promoting genocide in the Third World because of his refusal to countenance the use of condoms to combat the spread of AIDS. Solzhenitsyn was called an intolerant Russian ayatollah and hardcore theocrat because he stood for a Russian national revival inspired by Christian principles.

Leaders can expect to be savaged by their opponents and the media. Naturally they will suffer, but they will also learn to smile. Endurance, born of fanatical opposition to virtue, produces peace of heart and mind and soul and a proper pride in having fought the good fight.

As Thomas More awaited execution for refusing to abandon his principles, his calm and cheerful demeanor impressed and moved his loved ones. This cheerfulness stemmed from his devotion to conscience and ultimately from his rock-solid faith. More's biographer Gerard Wegemer observes: "His good humor was not simply a matter of temperament. More's unusual calm and good humor came from his habitual attention to conscience, which enabled him to assess the particular demands of each situation while keeping his eyes focused on eternity."[5]

I have had the pleasure and honor of meeting personally with Pope John Paul II, Aleksandr Solzhenitsyn, Lech Walesa, and Jérôme Lejeune. Despite the vast suffering they had endured (or perhaps because of it), they radiated peace and joy. They evinced no hatred, no bitterness, no resentment. I met Solzhenitsyn at his dacha near Moscow when he was 85 years old and not in the best of health. I shall never forget his good cheer and infectious enthusiasm for life. Similarly, Lejeune's amazing serenity undoubtedly stemmed

---

5. G. Wegemer, *Thomas More, A Portrait of Courage.* New York: Scepter Publishers, 1995, pp. 222–223.

from his leonine courage. Some words he spoke could stand as an epitaph: "I am not fighting people; I am fighting false ideas." He who is capable of condemning sin while loving the sinner, of rejecting bad ideas but embracing those who propagate them, is well able to withstand personal attacks and retain his peace of mind.

BOLDNESS AND DARING

Leaders face evil with equanimity, but they do not hesitate to destroy it the moment they have the chance. To do so, they must be bold, and constantly on guard.

When Lech Walesa threw down the gauntlet to the Kremlin by founding the Solidarity trade union, he had the support of John Paul II and Ronald Reagan. While that support was critical to Solidarity's eventual success, it would have counted for little had it not been for Walesa's boldness and readiness to do battle.

"A quality common to leaders," says Bennis, "is a bias toward action. That is, leaders have the capacity to convert purpose and vision into action. It isn't enough just to have a great vision you can use to inspire people. It has to become manifest and real in some external way, and produce results. Most leaders are pragmatic dreamers and practical idealists."[6]

Courage entails the ability to run risks. "Free the imagination and encourage risk-taking," says François Michelin, "going to the limits in order to see what happens."[7]

Few appreciate the immense creative drive needed to set up a business from scratch. Once a business is up and running, it is easy to think anyone could have done it. But those

---

6. W. Bennis and J. Goldsmith, *op. cit.*, preface and p. 4.
7. See J. Couretas, *op. cit.*

who succeed at start-ups are rarely just anyone. They are usually people of character and talent who are willing to run risks and act decisively.

Leaders persist in the face of obstacles, whether internal (i.e., stemming from their own defects) or external (i.e., having to do with objective factors beyond their control). They bring their projects to a proper conclusion, taking care to get the details right. Their perseverance is not pig-headedness but principled steadfastness.

Robert Schuman and Jean Monnet, for example, devoted their lives to convincing politicians of all stripes, one by one, day after day, of the urgent need for a fully integrated Europe. They were defiant in the face of setbacks. Escrivá persevered in his apostolic activities throughout the Spanish Civil War, even as churches were being burned and clerics arrested, tortured, and killed.

Leaders realize their dreams through constancy in work, not through dazzling words or gestures. They are strong, but they know how and when to be discreet. And they possess the virtue of self-control, which guarantees mastery of heart and mind. To this important virtue we now turn our attention.

Self-control
Mastery of Heart and Mind

> I no longer teach the management of people
> at work. . . . I am teaching, above all, how to
> manage oneself.
>
> — *PETER DRUCKER*

IF YOU WANT TO LEAD OTHERS, you must first be able to lead yourself. You need to possess the virtue of self-control or *temperance*, which subordinates passions (emotions and feelings) to the spirit and directs them towards the fulfillment of the mission at hand.

Self-control goes hand in hand with humility. It creates in the leader's heart room for other people and for the ideal of service. Intemperate people hesitate to serve and are often self-centered.

The virtue of self-control is often neglected in leadership literature. This reflects the culture of our time, with its emphasis on sensual pleasure and material comfort. Self-control is counter-cultural. It takes courage to talk about it. Moreover, we often conceive of leadership as a public role quite divorced from our private, intimate lives. Nothing could be further from the truth.

We need only think about the consequences of intemperance to understand why leaders need self-control.

Intemperance harms the intellect by obscuring the light of reason. The person given over to the pursuit of power, money, or pleasure loses contact with objective reality. "Unchaste abandon and the self-surrender of the soul to the world of sensuality," writes Pieper, "paralyzes the primordial powers of the moral person: the ability to perceive, in silence, the call of reality, and to make, in the retreat of this silence, the decision appropriate to the concrete situation of concrete action. This is the meaning inherent in all those propositions which speak of the falsification and corruption of prudence, of the blindness of the spirit, and of the splitting of the power of decision."[1]

Intemperance harms the will. It undermines courage (the capacity to stay the course) and justice: someone who craves power, money, or pleasure is hardly likely to take into account the common good or respect the dignity of those he deals with.

Intemperance, above all, harms the heart, because it crowds out magnanimity and humility. Obsessed with his power, pleasures, and possessions, the intemperate person conceives of life as an agglomeration of sensations. He loses all sense of mission and all capacity for serving others. He shrivels in stature virtually before our very eyes.

Intemperance undermines trust. Escrivá illustrates the point with this parable: "When you were children, you may have heard the fable of the farmer who was given a golden

---

1. J. Pieper, *Fortitude and Temperance*. p. 63.

pheasant. When the initial delight and surprise were over, the new owner began looking for a place where he could keep the pheasant. After several hours of doubting and changing his mind, he decided to put the pheasant in the hen house. The hens greatly admired the handsome new-comer and flocked round him with all the astonishment that might accompany the discovery of a demigod. While all this commotion was going on, feeding time came round and, as the farmer threw in the first handfuls of grain, our pheasant, who was starving after all the waiting, jumped greedily at the chance of filling his empty stomach. When they saw such vulgarity, their handsome hero gobbling down his food as hungrily as the commonest of birds, his disillusioned barn-yard companions fell to pecking their fallen idol until they had plucked out all his feathers."[2]

If my boss gets angry when contradicted, or envious when others outshine him, or hits the bottle, or treats women disrespectfully, I will soon lose confidence in him. I will go along with the atmosphere he is creating if I am a coward, or praise him if I am a fool, but I will not consider him a leader. Like the barnyard animals that turned on the vain pheasant, I will regard him with contempt.

In practice, people do not distinguish between a leader's professional abilities and his personal behavior, even if they say otherwise. They are deeply put off by double standards.

Self-control has a direct influence on how leaders carry out their professional duties. Consider the matter of time management. Leaders know they must devote sufficient time to their most important functions: long-term planning, the professional and moral education of staff, motivating colleagues,

2. J. Escrivá, *Friends of God*, no. 113.

etc. Yet surveys indicate that leaders rarely spend more than ten percent of their time on such vital functions. They tend to do what they like rather than what they ought. This is a natural human weakness. It is also a failure of the virtue of self-control.

Harry Truman had enough self-control to give up concentrating on domestic affairs (what he liked to do) and instead concentrate on foreign affairs (what he had to do). He launched the Marshall plan that rescued Western Europe. By contrast Lyndon Johnson had not enough self-control to stop concentrating on his domestic policies (what he liked to do) and instead concentrate on the Vietnam War (what he had to do). As a result he lost both the Vietnam War and the domestic reforms.[3]

We usually *like* to deal with urgent matters. "Urgent matters," says Covey, "are usually visible. They press on us; they insist on action. . . . They're usually right in front of us. And often they are pleasant, easy, fun to do. But so often they are unimportant! *Importance*, on the other hand, has to do with results. If something is important, it contributes to your mission, your values, your high priority goals."[4] How often have we seen the boss frantically attending to "urgent business" that proves to be trivial?

Many people in leadership roles fail to control their passions. Seminars on time management, however sophisticated, are no solution because the problem for such people is not technical in nature but moral. They need to learn to control their passions. They need to learn to say "No."

---

3. See P. Drucker, *Management Challenges for the 21st Century*, HarperCollins 2001, p. 182.
4. S. Covey, *The 7 Habits of Highly Effective People*. p. 151.

DIRECTION, RATHER THAN REPRESSION

Plato considered the body to be the tomb of the soul and likened passions to chains that enslave it. He believed man must free himself from the tyranny of passions by transcending the material world and entering the realm of the spirit. For Plato, human freedom means freedom from matter.

But the human body is as much God's creation as the human soul, and the passions a valid expression of our God-given human nature. It follows that curbing passions by renouncing material reality is not the way to go. What is required instead is the subordination of passions to reason by means of the virtue of self-control.

Human beings are made up of both body and soul. It follows that what is purely spiritual ceases to be fully human. Passions are the wellspring that sustain and vivify human nature. The human virtues presuppose passions. Thus, Platonism—and with it stoicism and Puritanism—fail to grasp human nature in the richness of its totality.

Passions, therefore, must not be repressed, but rather directed by and subordinated to the mind. Self-control becomes, in Pieper's words, "the shore, the banks, from whose solidity the stream receives the gift of straight, unhindered course, of force, descent, and velocity."[5]

THE POWER OF PURITY

Sexuality is a gift from God. Its aim is love and *pro-creation*. Seeing sex mainly as an instrument of personal gratification and acting accordingly introduces moral chaos into the very core of one's being. Unfortunately, this is what many people do these days.

---

5. J. Pieper, *op. cit.*, p. 82.

Modern culture has become thoroughly over-sexualized. Vast and growing numbers of men and women practice contraception and consume pornography with dangerous consequences for their own personalities as they become increasingly incapable of normal human emotions.

Writing in the early years of the sexual revolution, the late Austrian psychiatrist Viktor Frankl noted the first signs of a phenomenon that has since become ubiquitous—the tendency of husbands to instrumentalize wives, and vice versa, with sexual stimulation often supplanting love as the essence of marriage.

This state of affairs can and usually does drive a wedge between spouses. "I was astonished at the origin of our hostility," acknowledges the main character of Tolstoy's *The Kreutzer Sonata*, a newlywed whose marriage enshrines the pleasures of the flesh and nothing else. "And yet how clear it was! This hostility is nothing but a protest of human nature against the beast that enslaves it. It could not be otherwise. This hatred was the hatred of accomplices in a crime."[6]

To paraphrase the Spanish writer Pío Baroja, man is convinced he is just a millimeter above the ape; as a result, he behaves as if he were a centimeter below the pig. Consequently, the integrity of culture is called into question, threatening society itself with slow-motion collective suicide.

Thus, the meaning of Aristotle's dictum that self-control is true "self love"[7] becomes clear. The virtue of self-control shields our interior lives, and society itself, from the forces of chaos and destruction.

---

6. L. Tolstoy, *The Kreutzer Sonata*. chapter 13. Kila, MT: Kessinger Publishing Co., 2005.
7. Aristotle, *Nicomachean Ethics*, 9, 8.

Yet the virtue of self-control is more than this. It contains within it the virtue of purity, which Escrivá calls "a *decisive affirmation* on the part of the will in love."[8] Purity helps us to forget ourselves and to remain focused on God, and on other people and their needs.

Purity, as a radical and powerful demonstration of selflessness, predisposes the leader to be open to others and to serve them fearlessly, joyfully, and without calculation.

DETACHMENT: MASTERY OF THE SPIRIT

In addition to purity, self-control contains within it the virtue of detachment—from money, power, one's good name, and all manner of worldly things.

These things may be objectively good, but they are not fitting goals or ends in themselves. I will become the slave of whichever one I choose, and will live in fear of losing it or seeing its value diminished.

Detachment has nothing to do with being materially rich or poor. It is a quality of spirit. It can be practiced even in the midst of abundance.

Detachment, like any other virtue, is embodied in leaders of strong individuality, men and women who differ in mentality, spirit, and temperament, yet are one in their quest for interior greatness. All are called to practice detachment at the highest level. The CEO of a Fortune 500 company is called to live detachment just as surely as a Franciscan friar. This does not mean showing up at the office in sackcloth and sandals. But his calling to be detached is no less real and no less urgent.

---

8. J. Escrivá, *Christ Is Passing By*, no. 25. New York: Scepter Publishers, 2002.

"Detachment," in Escrivá's words, "is not a noisy and showy beggarliness, nor is it a mask for laziness and neglect. You should dress in accordance with the demands of your social standing, your family background, your work. . . . Do everything with naturalness, without being extravagant."[9]

Detachment means keeping the things we use in good condition, making them last, and getting the best out of them. When Robert Schuman was France's Minister of Finance, he followed a policy of fiscal austerity to help France recover from the economic strains of the Second World War. He set the example himself: in the evenings he switched off the lights in the offices and corridors of the Ministry of Finance. On weekends, he traveled from Paris to his home in Lorraine without reserving a whole train compartment for himself, even though he was entitled to do so. He stood in line to buy his rail ticket like everyone else. "Let's not despise little savings," he said. "The sum of little savings makes great economies."[10]

Detachment, like purity, is mastery of the heart. These are the wings on which leaders ascend to the heights, like eagles.

A TIME FOR MEEKNESS AND A TIME FOR WRATH

Self-control applies to the gamut of emotions, including wrath. Leaders do not readily lose their cool. They remain serene even in the most trying of circumstances and do not hesitate to treat those around them with respect and even gentleness.

---

9. J. Escrivá, *Friends of God*, no. 122.
10. See R. Lejeune, *op. cit.*, chap. 13.

"In the feverish atmosphere of parliamentary debates," wrote the French Socialist Deputy André Philip, "it was refreshing to find a man like Schuman always ready for dialogue, trying to persuade and taking into account objections, always with the same serenity and courtesy. He never used vulgar means, never exaggerated the weight of an argument, never raised his voice."[11]

If you practice meekness, even your fiercest opponents will begin to listen, however reluctantly. And people will regard you with affection when you respond to their shortcomings not with angry rebukes but with objective advice offered in a spirit of charity.

Though "wrath" often connotes a vengeful rage and is certainly a bad thing, there is such a thing as *righteous wrath*—in the face of injustice, for example. Jesus Christ displayed righteous wrath when he drove the moneychangers out of the temple with a whip.

Robert Schuman, a peaceful man by temperament, showed his claws in opposing the French Republic's attempt to abolish religious education in Alsace and Lorraine, then newly restored to French jurisdiction after the First World War. Although a young deputy in the National Assembly, Schuman rose to his feet and thundered, "Secularized schools are a scheme to de-Christianize France. We reject them." The government beat a hasty retreat.

Righteous wrath has a symbiotic relationship with courage, whereas "self-control" in the face of injustice often disguises cowardice. A desire for peace in our time is not a bad thing, but if it conceals cowardice in the face of injustice, all manner of evil can flow from it.

---

11. See R. Lejeune, *op. cit.*, Prologue 2.

GRATITUDE VS. ENVY

Envy is a big obstacle on the path towards leadership. It makes people behave in small, unpleasant and sometimes ugly ways.

Envy is *not* the ambition to possess as much as my neighbor possesses or to be as gifted as he is. Such an ambition can be a healthy thing and usually indicates an inclination to leadership. Envy is something else. It involves bitterness and resentment, possibly combined with a desire to bring down one's neighbor. It can easily become a toxic brew engendering hatred. Often, it has its roots in an inferiority complex.

Envy is the product of small-mindedness. The envious person is convinced that earthly goods (material, cultural, and spiritual) are finite and cannot be shared.

There is no place for envy in a leader's heart. Leaders practice the virtue of gratitude, which is the opposite of envy. They say "thank you" and reward people for their efforts.

STUDIOSITAS VS. CURIOSITAS

Leaders are studious, not curious. The Latin words *studiositas* and *curiositas* signify temperate and intemperate desires for knowledge, respectively. *Studiositas* is the desire to know in order to perceive reality and understand the nature of things. *Curiositas* is the desire to know for the pleasure it gives. As such, it represents a kind of spiritual promiscuity. The Russian poet Marina Tsvetaeva called intellectuals carried away by curiosity "brainy sensualists."

Leaders strive to improve their level of culture. True culture is much more than a superficial knowledge of many things. Pedantry, rote memorization, and novelties are useless. Certainly we need information, but we also need to know what to make of it once we have it. We need time to reflect. We need a moral framework that will help us make sense of disparate facts and ideas. We must become adept at separating out the true and the beautiful from the chaff of the false and nonsensical. This is *studiositas*, as opposed to mere *curiositas*.

Leaders do not read just any books or magazines, watch just any films, or listen to just any music. Aware of their own dignity as human beings, they filter out that which is morally dubious and fill their hearts and minds with that which is noble. They have a plan for building up their personalities and those of their followers. They know that in devising such a plan they must be selective, and that means practicing the virtue of self-control.

CONCLUSION

If we do not cultivate self-control, our desire to serve will soon dwindle to nothing. Obsessed with our pleasures and possessions, we will lose sight of those around us and forget all about noble undertakings, as there will be nothing noble about us.

Certainly, we must learn to say "no" to all that is base and useless. But that is not the end of the story. We must say "yes" to that which is true and noble, the very trait we develop when we practice magnanimity. Far from being something pinched and puritanical, self-control is the vital pre-condition for the flourishing of the soul that is magnanimity.

CHAPTER 4

Justice

Communion and Communication

> Justice is a pious attention to everything.
> — *VYACHESLAV IVANOV*

THE LAST VIRTUE WE WILL CONSIDER IS JUSTICE—the habit of giving others their due, not merely now and then, but always. The just man is committed to doing good as he goes about faithfully fulfilling his professional, familial, social, and religious responsibilities.

Justice—like prudence, courage, and self-control—governs man's efforts to order his interior self. But unlike those virtues, it also governs his relations with the community. Justice is about man's dealings with others. It is more than a legal or social science concept; it is a personal virtue, a quality of character.

Many consider themselves just because they obey the law, pay their taxes, and support charitable organizations to alleviate poverty and other social ills. These things are admirable, but, as we shall see, there is much more to justice.

HUMAN NATURE IS IMMUTABLE

The very notion that one's neighbor has a *due*—that he is due something merely by virtue of the fact that he exists—implies that the neighbor has rights. But rights cannot be firmly established in the absence of a concept of man and human nature grounded in reason.

If we do not have a concept of man rooted in reason, we will soon find ourselves living in a world devoid of rights, and therefore of justice—the world of Auschwitz and Kolyma.[1]

Human nature is not an illusion. It is not an abstract, possibly unreal, mental construct, something esoteric. It exists. It is intelligible and embodies immutable principles, which are self-evident natural laws.

Not even the totalitarian states of modern times succeeded in abolishing human nature, although that was not for want of trying. Now liberal, democratic states are getting into the act.

In the summer of 1983, I made my first trip to the Soviet Union to visit relatives in the southern republic of Georgia. I stayed with my great-aunt Elena. She had been living alone with her son since 1938 when the Communist secret police shot her husband and two of her three brothers. Her third brother had fled the Soviet Union in 1928 and had settled in

---

1. A remote, scarcely habitable sub-region of the Russian Far East four times the size of France, Kolyma was the site of scores of the Soviet Gulag's most atrocious slave labor camps. More than a million prisoners, mostly Russians, died extracting gold, uranium, and other raw materials from the frozen earth. Kolyma was, in the words of Solzhenitsyn, "the pole of ferocity of that amazing country of Gulag." Like Auschwitz, the Nazi extermination camp in which two million people, mostly Jews, perished, Kolyma has become a byword for man's inhumanity to man and the moral bankruptcy of Godless ideological systems.

Paris where he married Madeleine Ducrocq, the daughter of a French general. His name was Artchil Gedevanishvili. He was my maternal grandfather.

Aunt Elena introduced me to Sandro, a distant cousin I had never met. Like me, he was 21 years old and a university student. We became good friends and decided to spend a few days together at the Black Sea resort of Batumi, where we rented an apartment in a dilapidated house. By day, it offered a fine view of the sea and the town. By night, sleep proved impossible because somewhere in the gloaming an old woman wailed incessantly over the grave of her son in some unseen cemetery. So Sandro and I grabbed a bottle of Georgian wine and a pack of Russian cigarettes and took up residence on the balcony where we held forth on life, death, and eternity into the wee hours.

To my surprise, I discovered that Sandro, although born and raised in the Soviet Union, shared many of my own fundamental moral and human values. In his orthodox Marxist education and as a member of the Komsomol (the Communist youth organization), Sandro had heard nothing of God or the spirit or human nature or love. Instead, they filled his head with class struggle, the preeminence of matter, and the scientific nature of socialism. Nevertheless, Sandro had retained a sense of man and his true nature, as if it were innate. I began to understand that a sense of man precedes education and is capable of resisting even the most virulent propaganda.

The temptation to "liberate" human beings from their own nature is not something unique to Marxism, but is common to all secular materialist worldviews. Philosophers such as Nietzsche, Sartre, and de Beauvoir refused to acknowledge that human nature, as such, even existed. For them, everything was reducible to human will. Reason counted for nothing.

More recently, Elisabeth Badinter, a writer and wife of a former French Minister of Justice, asserted the urgent necessity of *liberating women from womanhood* by developing an incubator that would gestate a child for nine months, and of *liberating men from manhood* by developing technologies that would allow men to conceive a child and give birth to it by Caesarean section.[2] Badinter's denial of a biological nature is fashionably *au courant*. It is also totalitarian in spirit, a project worthy of the quack Soviet biologist Lysenko.[3] As such it has no future, although it is certainly capable of wreaking lots of havoc before people see through it.

Where the immutability of human nature is called into question, human rights cannot exist. Human rights are sacrosanct only because they are inscribed in our (immutable) human natures. They can be enshrined in such international conventions as the 1948 Universal Declaration of Human Rights, but they do not derive from such sources. They transcend parliaments and courts and tribunals.

The assault on the once-inviolable right to life began in earnest only after modern society began casting doubt on the existence of an immutable human nature. The innocent and defenseless victims of abortion and euthanasia have paid, and continue to pay, the supreme price for society's

---

2. See *Architects of the Culture of Death*. pp. 196–197.

3. Trofim Denisovich Lysenko (1898–1976) was the charlatan Soviet biologist who dominated the USSR's scientific establishment under Stalin. His rejection of modern genetics, which he considered a "bourgeois pseudo-science," did grave and lasting harm to Soviet and then Russian agriculture. His name is a byword for quackery, incompetence, and the damage that occurs when ideology takes precedence over objective reality and the natural order.

errant ways. Some have called the West's regnant political ideology "democratic totalitarianism."

All too often justice and democracy do not mix; sometimes majorities abridge or even crush human rights: The United States had legalized slavery from Washington to Lincoln; Hitler was democratically elected; many Western intellectuals treated Marxism as gospel truth for much of the twentieth century despite incontrovertible evidence of its failure east of the Berlin Wall.

Justice means that people have fundamental rights, which, as we have noted, stem not from fleeting social arrangements, but from immutable human nature. They are grounded in reason, and are thus impervious to the shifting winds of public opinion. This is the golden rule of ethics: "Reason first; the will second."

STRIVING FOR THE COMMON GOOD

Human beings are individuals, not atoms of self-interest. They are social beings that live and thrive in communion with others. If my community flourishes, I flourish; if it does not, neither do I. I strive for the common good.

If I were to turn my back on the community, I would not develop as a human being. Individualism, which is indistinguishable from egoism, is the enemy of healthy individuality. "True individuality," writes Russian philosopher Vladimir Soloviev, "is an expression of all-unity, a means of perceiving and assimilating all else to one's self. In affirming himself outside of all else, man thereby deprives his own existence of meaning, removes from himself the true substance of life, and transforms his individuality into an empty form. In this way, egoism is in no way self-consciousness and the self-affirmation of individuality, but rather its self-negation and death."[4]

Leaders are individuals, not individualists. They interact with the community in ways beneficial to both. They do not confuse community with the collective, as exponents of the Enlightenment are prone to do. They see the community as made up of human beings, real and personal in their individual uniqueness, and not as an amalgam of faceless "masses" or antagonistic social classes.

Leaders strive for the common good, which, for them is something whose importance transcends the Gross National Product and other indicators of prosperity. It also transcends government-sponsored welfare programs for the indigent, as necessary as they may be. The common good entails nothing less than the building of a society in which each and every individual can achieve *moral perfection and material welfare.* The common good comprises respect for truth, freedom, education, work, family, property, religion, human rights, culture, health, and the law.

Leaders promote the common good not through lip service, but through the faithful fulfillment of their professional, social, religious, and family responsibilities.

FAITHFULLY FULFILLING ONE'S ORDINARY RESPONSIBILITIES

Leaders strive for perfection in work. Two thousand years ago, Plotinius said that justice simply means "doing one's own work" and fulfilling "one's own task."[5]

---

4. See V. Soloviev, *The Meaning of Love*, II, 3. Translation by the author.
5. Plotinius, *Enneads*, I, 2, 6. Cited by Pieper, *Justice*. New York: Pantheon Books, 1955, p. 46.

Leaders work with the greatest possible professional competence. They *sanctify* their work—they make it holy—by transforming it into prayer, and thereby, in Escrivá's words, "transforming the prose of this life into poetry, into heroic verse."[6]

Leaders conceive of work as service to all. Again, Escrivá: "You cannot think of others as if they were digits, or rungs on a ladder on which you can rise, or a multitude to be harangued or humiliated, praised or despised, according to circumstances. Be mindful of what others are—and first of all those who are at your side: children of God, with all the dignity that marvelous title entails."[7]

Leaders are devoted to family life. Love for work and "workaholism" are two different things. If I allow my work to cause me to neglect my family, I have a deeply flawed understanding of justice.

Thomas More, Pyotr Stolypin, Karl von Habsburg, and Jérôme Lejeune were wonderful husbands and fathers. In researching a book on senior corporate executives, Warren Bennis was not surprised to discover that nearly all were still married to their original spouses.

Leaders, guided by prudence, understand what to do when conflicts arise between professional and family commitments. There are no magic formulas for getting it right, but if your motto is "family first" and you live by it, you are on the right track. A senior executive of my acquaintance once attended a board meeting that went on interminably, the result of poor planning. Finally, around 8:00 p.m., he announced to his colleagues, "Friends, I have to go. My wife and children are waiting for me. I can change my job if I have to, but I

---

6. J. Escrivá, *Furrow*, no. 500. New York: Scepter Publishers, 2002.
7. J. Escrivá, *Christ Is Passing By*, no. 36.

can't change my wife and kids." And with that he left the room. There was shocked silence, but my friend had given his colleagues a good lesson in living the virtues of prudence and justice.

Leaders see family life as a source of strength, not an obstacle. Janne Haaland Matlary, Norway's former State Secretary for Foreign Affairs, explains the significance of parenthood in leadership: "The maturity that parents must gain simply because they are parents involved in their children's lives—in terms of work and responsibility—is an incredibly valuable asset for a business leader with some perspective on what he is doing. Young, aggressive men, obsessed with profit seeking, are hardly the long-term human capital a sound business really wants. One needs trust, cultured interaction, and genuine interpersonal respect in order to lead."[8]

The extraordinary career of Cory Aquino is a case in point. When she was campaigning to oust Ferdinand Marcos from the presidency, the old dictator accused her of being unfit to govern because she was a housewife. But this housewife went on to win the election, send Marcos into exile, and thoroughly transform the Philippines.

Leaders practice the virtue of citizenship. They make their presence felt in the political, social, and cultural life of the community and the nation. Not all leaders have a political vocation, but as citizens and people of influence they cannot be indifferent to the political trends of the times, especially when they are so fraught with moral consequences.

---

8. J. Haaland Matlary, "Motherhood and Leadership: Professional Life on Women's Terms," address to a conference of the European Center for Leadership Development, Helsinki, November 9, 2001.

Leaders worship the Creator. Being humble, leaders know that life is a gift from God and that indifference to God is a grave injustice. If God willed my existence, justice requires that I love Him with all of my heart, all of my mind, and all of my soul. To worship God requires praying to Him, thanking Him, obeying the Ten Commandments and practicing the virtues they prescribe. How often have we met people who proclaim their faith in God, but seem less than intent on practicing, say, detachment, purity, or justice? They may have lots of great personal qualities, but they are tragically unable or unwilling to "live out" their faith.

The leader who sincerely practices his faith generates trust. He feels responsible for his leadership before God, not just the board of directors, Congress, or the court of public opinion. As G. K. Chesterton once said: "If I did not believe in God, I should still want my doctor, my lawyer, and my banker to do so." Yes, and my boss, too.

Justice goes hand-in-hand with humility. Faithfully to fulfill one's professional, social, religious, and family responsibilities requires overcoming one's ego. The proud man is not aware of what he owes others, only what others owe him. The humble man, by contrast, is aware of his responsibilities before God and man. He lives to serve.

Justice is also related to magnanimity. If we are to fulfill our ordinary duties perfectly, we need a visionary sense of the ordinary. We must be convinced that we will either find greatness in the context of humdrum reality and in service to the people we deal with every day or we will not find it at all.

JUSTICE AND TRUTH

Justice is intimately related to the virtue of truthfulness and, as we shall see in the next section, to the virtue of charity.

Leaders tell the truth. Truth resides in the conformity between what we think and how things are. It requires humility on the leader's part to understand that he is not the measure of all things. He needs to recognize the reality existing outside of his own mind and to consider the laws of nature, both physical and moral, as more than matters of opinion.

Truthfulness requires courage—the courage to stand for moral truth, even if this means contradicting political correctness and provoking a reaction.

Leaders *always* desire peace, but never peace at any price. A peace based on falsehood is no peace at all. The prime example in modern times was the notorious Munich Agreement of 1938 ratifying Nazi Germany's claim to a section of neighboring Czechoslovakia—the Sudetenland—that had a large German-speaking population. On the strength of Adolph Hitler's personal assurances that he had no further territorial ambitions beyond the Sudetenland, British Prime Minister Neville Chamberlain and his French counterpart Edouard Daladier signed the fateful document. Then they returned to their respective capitals in triumph, proclaiming "peace in our time!" Both Chamberlain and Daladier knew perfectly well that the Munich Agreement enshrined a falsehood. With the cheers of Parisians ringing in his ears, Daladier confided to an aide: "Idiots, if only they knew what's in store for them!" Daladier was a coward, and he knew the price of his cowardice: within two years the *Wehrmacht* was marching down the Champs Elysées.

Unlike Chamberlain and Daladier, Pope Pius XI and his immediate successor Pius XII spoke the truth about Hitler and the nature of his regime. In 1937 Pius XI condemned Nazism in no uncertain terms in his German-language encyclical letter *Mit brennender Sorge* ("With Burning Anxiety"). The letter was read from the pulpits of Catholic churches throughout Germany, much to Hitler's consternation.

In 1941 and 1942 the *New York Times* ran editorials praising Pius XII, for his moral courage. It extolled his "lonely voice crying out of the silence of a continent" against "the violent occupation of territory, and the exile and persecution of human beings, for no other reason than race."

Albert Einstein paid tribute to Pius XII as early as 1940, saying that in Germany "only the Catholic Church stood squarely across the path of Hitler's campaign for suppressing the truth." After the war, numerous Jewish organizations praised the Pope. Rome's Chief Rabbi, Israel Zolli, converted to Catholicism and chose to be baptized Eugenio—Pius XII's given name—in tribute to the Roman Pontiff. He cited Pius' witness to religious fraternity as one of the factors leading to his conversion. Remembering the Pope shortly after his death in 1958, Israeli Foreign Minister Golda Meir praised his courage in resisting the Nazis: "When fearful martyrdom came to our people in the decade of Nazi terror, the voice of the pope was raised for the victims. The life of our times was enriched by a voice speaking out on the great moral truths above the tumult of daily conflict."[9]

Indeed, the Papacy's forthright opposition to ideologies that threaten human dignity accounts for much of its considerable prestige in modern times. Leo XIII's *Rerum*

9. See Rabbi David G. Dalin, *The Myth of Hitler's Pope: How Pope Pius XII Rescued Jews from the Nazis*. Washington, D.C.: Regnery Publishing, 2005.

Novarum (1891) reminds supporters of both liberal capitalism and collectivistic socialism that the economy exists to serve people, not people the economy. John Paul II's *Evangelium Vitae* (1995) warns the West that its culture of death is offensive to God and threatens its very survival.

These encyclical letters have generated enormous trust in the Catholic Church. Many have come to realize that the Catholic Church possesses a profound, universal voice that rises above the secular powers-that-be, including money, intellectual fashion and the Babel of competing ideologies. This voice is ever willing to speak the truth and rise to the defense of those whose human rights are being attacked by totalitarian ideologies of whichever stripe—dictatorial or democratic.

Leaders strive for sincerity and simplicity. The former is telling the unvarnished truth about your thoughts, feelings, and desires; the latter avoids all affectation, officiousness, pedantry, and boasting. Sincerity is expressed in words, simplicity in actions. Both are inseparable from truthfulness.

Simplicity means doing away with the dichotomy between our interior selves and the face we show to the world. Simplicity precludes "acting." Ronald Reagan, the Hollywood actor, always remained just who he was—small town America's native son—even as President of the United States. Thanks to his essential devotion to truth—a sign of character—he stayed remarkably natural despite his years in Tinsel Town. Politicians less concerned with serving the common good than with preserving their own power tend to forfeit simplicity. The longer they continue in that vein, the more complicated they become and the more prone to acting than ever Reagan was.

JUSTICE AND CHARITY

Leaders respect the dignity of others, including their right to be told the truth, trusted, treated fairly, and rewarded and thanked for a job well done. Thus, they give people their due. Indeed, they do more than this:

Leaders, steeped in justice and humility, understand that life is a gift from God, and are therefore willing to . . . give . . . even if there is no strict obligation to do so.

We do not, strictly speaking, owe kindness, friendship, or love to others, nor do others have a right to demand them of us. But the deeper our knowledge of man, the better we understand what treating others justly means.

"Precisely because man is a personal being," wrote John Paul II, "it is not possible to fulfill our duty towards him [i.e., give him his due, the very definition of justice] except by loving him."[10] Not justice *or* love, but justice *with* love.

Love means perceiving your neighbor as "another self." This perception calls forth the important leadership qualities of empathy, friendship, cheerfulness, and mercy.

Leaders demonstrate empathy by treating each person as a unique individual. They are aware of and show respect for his or her needs, temperament, cultural background, family situation, and other personal circumstances. Organizations run by people with a weak understanding of and commitment to justice tend to be cold and impersonal.

Leaders are cheerful and cultivate friendship. Although not immune to the vicissitudes of life, leaders are always cheerful, thanks to their firm determination to serve others. The surest way to get down in the dumps is to become

---

10. John Paul II, *Memory and Identity*. London: Weidenfeld & Nicolson, 2005, p. 150.

wrapped up in your own ego; the surest way to be happy is to forget yourself—that is to say, serve others.

"Cheerfulness," writes Escrivá, "does not mean the jingling of bells, or the gaiety of a dance at the local hall. True cheerfulness is something deeper, something within: something that keeps us peaceful and happy, though at times our face may be stern."[11]

Thomas More gave us a brilliant example of cheerfulness and friendship—two inseparable virtues. Here is a portrait of More by his friend Erasmus:

> "His countenance is in harmony with his character, being always expressive of an amiable joyousness, and even an incipient laughter and, to speak candidly, it is better framed for gladness than for gravity or dignity, though without any approach to folly or buffoonery. . . . He seems born and framed for friendship, and is a most faithful and enduring friend. . . . When he finds anyone sincere and according to his heart, he so delights in their society and conversation as to place in it the principal charm of life. . . . In a word, if you want a perfect model of friendship, you will find it in no one better than in More."[12]

Friendship is in crisis in the modern world. Many fear friendship because they fear the duties that flow from it. In consequence, they back off from becoming bound or committed to anyone. They cultivate *relationships* instead of friends. They smile and joke, but they have no real interest in people. Leaders, by contrast, are adept at making friends because they are driven by the desire to serve. Friendship, indeed, is another name for service.

---

11. J. Escrivá, *The Forge*, no. 520. New York: Scepter Publishers, 2002.
12. Erasmus, Letter to Ulrich von Hutten, 23 July 1519.

Finally, leaders are merciful. They forgive easily. They do not indulge evil, but rather strive to bring the evildoer to a conversion of heart. Jesus Christ did not judge the woman caught in adultery, but instead corrected her, saying, "Go, and do not sin again."[13]

To be merciful does not mean tolerating behavior that harms other people, either individually or collectively. For example, managers may have to dismiss employees whose activities are detrimental to the organization, and who refuse to mend their ways. The leader who fails to remove the wrong people from positions of influence on the grounds of mercy is not showing mercy to those who will suffer from his decision. His higher responsibility is to the general welfare of the organization and the people who work there.

Leaders, as noted in the introduction to this book, lead through the auctoritas (authority) that stems from character; but they do not hesitate, when necessary, to resort to the *potestas* (power) inherent in their position. If they fail to discipline subordinates, they will soon lose authority.

"Justice and mercy are so united," says Thomas Aquinas, "that the one ought to be mingled with the other; justice without mercy is cruelty; mercy without justice is the mother of dissolution."[14]

Empathy, cheerfulness, friendship, and mercy are virtues of *communion*. They give rise to communication in the deepest sense because they facilitate entry into the hearts and minds of others. Faulty justice—justice without love—means faulty communication.

_____

13. Jn 8:11.
14. Thomas Aquinas, Commentary on the Gospel of Matthew.

Whereas prudence emphasizes the need for *right reason* in leadership, justice emphasizes the need for *good will*, which is reflected not in mere desires or intentions, but in the constant determination to give everyone his due.

PART III

LEADERS ARE NOT BORN, THEY ARE TRAINED

In Part One we defined magnanimity and humility, the quintessential leadership virtues. In Part Two we considered the four cardinal virtues—prudence, courage, self-control, justice—which form the bedrock of leadership.

By now the reader must be wondering, "How can I acquire and develop these leadership virtues?" In this section we answer that question. But first we must say something about *aretology*, the science of virtue.

CHAPTER 1

Aretology

The Science of Virtue

> The Aristotelian system of virtues is clearly based
> upon a genuine anthropology. . . . This system, on
> which the self-realization of human freedom in truth
> depends, can be described as exhaustive. It is not
> an abstract or *a priori* system.
>
> —*JOHN PAUL II*

ARETOLOGY—THE SCIENCE OF VIRTUE—was founded by the classical Greek philosophers and enriched by its encounter with Judeo-Christian thought and spirituality. The name derives from *aretē*, the Greek word for virtue.

Aretology comprises two kinds of virtues: *intellectual* virtues related to human knowledge and *ethical* virtues related to human behavior. Intellectual virtues help us grasp reality, while ethical virtues help us act in accordance with human nature. Prudence has both qualities. It is both an *intellectual* virtue, inasmuch as it involves knowledge, and an *ethical* virtue, inasmuch as that knowledge is directed towards decision and action.

Ethical virtues are also called *human virtues* or *natural virtues*, to distinguish them from the divine or supernatural virtues of which Christian moral theology speaks. Plato defined the main human virtues as prudence, justice, courage, and self-control, though the poet Pindar and the playwright Æschylus had already spoken of them. Ambrose of Milan (fourth century A.D.) called them the *cardinal virtues*, because they are the *cardines*, "hinges," on which all other human virtues depend.

Greek philosophers, above all Plato and Aristotle, wrote about human virtues as did the Jews and the Romans, Cicero and Seneca the best known, followed by Christian writers, especially Augustine and Thomas Aquinas.

In modern times, a number of well-known writers have given sustained attention to this topic. Among the most influential are the philosopher Josef Pieper (Germany, 1904–1997), the priest and founder of the Roman Catholic lay organization Opus Dei, Saint Josemaría Escrivá (Spain/Italy, 1902–1975), management guru Peter Drucker (Austria/USA, 1909–2005), and the best-selling advocate of "principle-centered" leadership, Stephen R. Covey (USA, 1932–).

Josef Pieper builds on the foundations laid by Aristotle and Plato, Augustine and Aquinas. His strength is his capacity for penetrating the dense terminology of the classical past while expressing himself in a modern language of striking clarity and precision.

Josemaría Escrivá deals with human virtues from the practical point of view of an experienced pastor of souls. He sees them as vital to the sanctification of professional work, perhaps the overriding theme of his preaching and writing in his 50 years of priestly service.

Peter Drucker is the prophet of management *par excellence*. The whole of his teaching (conveyed in 31 books) is permeated with deep aretological considerations. Drucker once said, "All of those who have written about me have portrayed me as an author of business management and administration, which I am not."[1] That's right; he was a purveyor of aretology.

Stephen Covey writes about virtues from an essentially psychological point of view. His strength is his ability to demonstrate with attractive and telling anecdotes the relation between virtue and personal effectiveness.

---

1. Letter of P. Drucker to G. Stein, 1998. See "Peter Drucker," Mercatornet, Friday, 18 November 2005.

CHAPTER 2

We Are What We Habitually Do

Virtue comes about as a result of habit.

—*ARISTOTLE*

A VIRTUE IS A HABIT. Like any habit, it is acquired by *repetition*. If we repeatedly act courageously, we will eventually do so habitually. If we repeatedly act with humility, it will soon become our habitual way of behaving.

The necessity of repetition is sometimes short-circuited when people are thrust into circumstances—wartime, for example—that require heroic choices. Karol Wojtyla, the future Pope John Paul II, forged his character during the Nazi occupation of Poland, thereby undergoing a deep personal transformation. Other examples were the university students who became Escrivá's first followers in the years leading up to the Spanish Civil War. They achieved remarkable human maturity through the hardships of war, becoming pillars of strength that would sustain the growth of Opus Dei on five continents.

The more you practice a virtue, the more it becomes a stable part of your character. A person cannot fall out of a habit from one day to the next. One cowardly action does not make you a coward. "To become a villain, it is not enough to want it!" says Violaine to Pierre de Créon, characters in Paul Claudel's *The Tidings Brought to Mary*.

Virtuous living stabilizes behavior. One is less susceptible to external stimuli, less reactive, more in control of one's life. You act courageously, not just in extraordinary situations but routinely. Virtue is not a kind of talent, used as needed; it is ever-present in all circumstances. It becomes who you are; it is you.

"Yours is an unbalanced character," writes Escrivá. "You are a broken keyboard. You play very well on the high notes and on the low notes, but no sound comes from the ones in the middle, the ones used in ordinary life, the ones people normally hear."[1] Ordinary life—that is where virtue must be practiced habitually.

Because virtue is a habit, we must consider the lives of famous people in their totality before deciding which ones are worthy of emulation. Seek evidence of great deeds, to be sure, but more important, look for virtuous behavior in public and private life sustained over the course of a lifetime. Many people have achieved a few great deeds during their lifetime, but a *few* great deeds do not create virtue.

LEADERSHIP: A QUESTION OF CHARACTER, NOT TEMPERAMENT

Because leaders must be virtuous to be real leaders, and because virtue is a habit acquired through practice, we say "leaders are not born: they are trained."

---

1. J. Escrivá, *Furrow*, no. 440.

Leadership is a question of character, not temperament. Character is forged through training, but temperament is innate, a product of nature. It may aid the development of some virtues and hinder others. If I am passionate by nature, I may find it relatively easy to act boldly, and if I am reticent, I may find boldness a real challenge. Yet it is precisely because of my defects of temperament that I am so keenly aware of the need to struggle to overcome them. In this way defects are converted into moral strengths.

The virtues stamp character on our temperament so that temperament ceases to dominate us. If I lack virtues, I will be a slave to my temperament. Escrivá put it this way: "Don't say: 'That's the way I am ... it's my character.' It's your lack of character. . . ."[2]

Take control of your life. If you are irascible, practice self-control; if you are libidinous, practice purity. Do not become the slave of your defects.

Be aware that virtues regulate temperament. The impulsive person, inspired by the virtue of prudence, becomes more reflective. The anxious and hesitant person, inspired by the *same* virtue, is impelled to stop procrastinating and act. Virtues stabilize our personalities, banishing extreme manifestations.

Thus, temperament need not be an obstacle to leadership. The real obstacle is lack of character, which quickly leaves us drained of moral energy and quite incapable of leading. In other words, it robs us of our freedom.

---

2. J. Escrivá, *The Way*, no. 4.

THE CHALLENGE OF FREEDOM

We freely choose to be the kind of men and women we become. If we choose virtue, we will be men and women of character; if we choose vice, we will lead lives of sin; if we split the difference, as many do, we will be merely mediocre.

Childhood and adolescence have a big impact on our later choices. Our parents (should) influence us to discern good from evil and choose the former. But upbringing alone does not determine character. It is not uncommon that children raised in the same home come to use their freedom differently and thus turn out to be very different kinds of people. Ronald Reagan, for example, was utterly different from his brother Neil, two years his senior. They made different choices. Ronald set forth to conquer the world. Neil stayed at home in Illinois and worked in the insurance business. Ronald was an idealist. Neil's concerns were more mundane.

Freedom springs eternal and assures that we continue to grow even after we have entered adulthood. It is not unusual that grown-ups develop a longing to live virtuously and decide to acquire what may have passed them by in childhood.

Like temperament, our *cultural environment* may help or hinder the development of certain virtues. In a society given over to sensuality, it can be hard to cultivate the virtues of self-control and courage. In one that tends to produce people who are reticent and disinclined to say what they really think, it can be hard to practice sincerity. Where people recognize only empirical data as the basis for belief, it is hard to practice prudence.

It can be hard to live virtuously in today's cultural context, but it is by no means impossible. The ability to say "no" gives us great power. We are free to decide the extent to which we will allow the culture to affect us. If we opt for virtue, we will be able to take what is good and reject what is bad.

The more deeply we live the virtues, furthermore, the more likely it is that we will change the culture, rather than being content with merely shielding ourselves from its more pernicious effects. We must choose virtue—freely, consistently, joyously.

My grandmother is a case in point.

In 1920, three Russian sisters, Natasha, Ksenia, and Nina Anossova, followed their parents into self-imposed exile from Soviet Russia.[3] The family moved to Constantinople and then to Marseilles, before finally settling in Paris at the height of the Roaring '20s. Although the three sisters had received the same education at home in Saint Petersburg, each reacted in her own way to the libertine *Zeitgeist* that prevailed in the City of Light.

Natasha embraced hedonism: she married several rich businessmen in succession and enjoyed all of the considerable material comforts Paris had to offer.

Ksenia chose survival. Stricken with cancer, she eked out a humble existence overshadowed by the illness that took her life after ten years.

Nina embraced life as she found it. She met a young Russian emigrant who had lost his parents and his property in the civil war after the Bolshevik seizure of power. He came to France with nothing except his good name, a virtuous heart, and a desire to succeed. His name was Pavel Dianin-Havard. He and Nina were to become my paternal grandparents.

Nina and Pavel fell in love and married in Paris in 1926 and raised a family. Although they had a long, happy, and fruitful life, it could easily have been otherwise. Nina might

---

3. See N. Anossov, *Adieu Russie: Souvenirs*. Paris: Librairie des Cinq Continents, 1978.

have embraced the hedonism of Natasha or, like Ksenia, gone into survival mode. Instead *she chose life*, magnanimously serving family and friends, God and country, until her death at age 96.

Although the three sisters came to maturity in the same cultural environment—that of libertine Paris in the 1920s—each made her own distinctly different choice. Environment is not the main determinant of human destiny. Character is of decisive importance.

We have freely chosen to be what we are. Vice or virtue? It's up to us. Virtue implies and depends on freedom. It cannot be forced on us. It is something we freely choose. If we embrace the virtues and practice them assiduously, the path to leadership will be open. Leadership begins when we use our freedom responsibly.

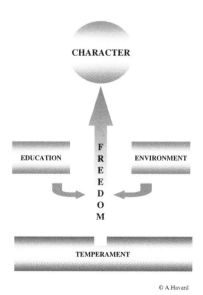

© A.Havard

CHAPTER 3

The Unity of All the Virtues

> Virtues grow together like the five fingers of
> the hand.
>
> —*THOMAS AQUINAS*

EACH OF THE MANY VIRTUES IS INTERWOVEN with all the others. Their common wellspring is the *practical good*—i.e., the *spiritual good as revealed in concrete situations.*

THE CONNECTEDNESS OF THE VIRTUES

In striving to develop one virtue, I develop all the others. Take self-control: If I can control my passions, I will find it easier to maintain the objectivity to make right decisions (prudence) and to have reserves of energy for (courageously) staying the course when the going gets tough. In addition, if my heart is cleared of inordinate attachments, I am more likely to dedicate myself (magnanimously) to noble tasks and (humbly) serve others.

Consider humility: If I am humble, I will attain the clarity of moral vision to perceive the many gifts I have received from God, which is the precondition for responding *magnanimously* to his generosity. In living humility, I put my own needs and wants, likes and dislikes, opinions and prejudices on the back burner in order to serve others better. This enhances my practice of the virtue of *prudence*, and also the virtue of *justice* by making me attentive to my responsibilities to God, family, and society.

Prudence embodies the unity of all the virtues in a special way: It shows me when courage, self-control, justice, humility, and magnanimity are called for, and how best to manifest them in the concrete circumstances of the moment. "Prudence," says Pieper, "is cause, root, mother, measure, precept, guide, and prototype of all ethical virtues."[1] Guided by prudence, I will always clearly distinguish courage from cowardice, magnanimity from small-mindedness, true humility from false humility, self-control from intemperance, and justice from injustice.

"Through prudence," says Escrivá, "a man learns to be daring without being rash. . . . His self-control is not insensitive or misanthropic; his justice is not harsh nor is his patience servile."[2]

Prudence is not mediocrity, it is not half way there but the summit, the culmination point.

If it is hard for me to practice dissimilar virtues at the same time, it is because my temperament inclines me in one direction or another. Leaders who are kind by temperament may find it difficult to show the firmness required by justice; leaders of firm resolve may hesitate to show the kindness that humility demands. But thanks to prudence, leaders are able in each concrete case to determine the best course of action. Robert Schuman is an example of this. He possessed both of these qualities, which often seem contradictory, to a high degree.

---

1. J. Pieper, *Prudence*. p. 20.
2. J. Escrivá, *Friends of God*, no. 87.

If none of the virtues can develop in the absence of prudence, likewise we may assert that prudence cannot develop without the remaining virtues.

We cited the famous phrase of Aristotle above: "The good man judges each class of things rightly, and in each the truth appears to him." Consequently, only he who possesses courage, justice, and self-control can be prudent. All of the virtues nurture prudence and in turn are nurtured by it. This is not a closed circle, but an ascending spiral of growth.

The indestructible unity of the virtues empowers me to cultivate ... *with ease* ... qualities I had never imagined existed, just as a rich man has no trouble becoming even richer. If I am magnanimous, I will not find it hard to practice humility, because I already possess that virtue potentially. Some people think magnanimity contradicts humility because they confuse magnanimity with egocentricity and humility with a milquetoast approach to life. In fact, as we have seen, magnanimity and humility are the touchstones of greatness.

© A.Havard

THE UNITY OF PUBLIC AND PRIVATE VIRTUE

There is no such thing as a virtuous nation, a virtuous family, or a virtuous organization. There are only virtuous individuals.

At the same time, nevertheless, virtue abhors individualism. No one becomes better in isolation from other people. If I am courageous, it is probably because I have seen manifestations of courage by my parents, friends, or colleagues. Moreover, when I do the courageous thing, I stimulate others to do the same. My self-improvement and the self-improvement of those around me are inextricably linked. Thus, when lived out in practice, every virtue has a social dimension.

That is why the dichotomy that ethicists often posit between private and public virtue is really quite misleading. They use "private virtue" to signify virtues that "order man in himself," such as prudence, courage, and self-control, and "public virtue" to indicate qualities pertaining to how the individual relates to society, such as justice. The distinction is unfortunate, because justice is inextricably linked to all the other virtues. If I am not prudent, courageous, and temperate, it is highly unlikely I will be just.

Many politicians, lacking courage, make a travesty of justice. Think of Pontius Pilate and his brand of justice: "I could find no substance in any of the charges you bring against him [Jesus of Nazareth] . . . so I will scourge him . . . !"[3] Here is the frightening logic of a coward.

But in order to be just, I need more than courage. I also need prudence and self-control. If I cannot prudently assess the reality of the situation I face, and if I am so intemperate that I let my passions run away with me, how can I arrive at

---

3. Lk 23:14, 16.

a just decision? It's hardly likely that I can. Consider the case of Herodias in the New Testament.[4] Given over to lust, she demanded the head of John the Baptist because he had the temerity to insist that she change her ways.

---

4. See Mk 6:14–29.

CHAPTER 4

Leaders of Mind, Will, and Heart

> Virtue is a capacity of the human spirit, of the
> human will, and also of the heart.
>
> —*JOHN PAUL II*

ARETOLOGY IS AN ANTHROPOLOGICAL SCIENCE comprising a holistic vision of man. In addition to explicating the virtues, it aims to inculcate them through the formation of the intellect, the will, and the heart.

Human virtues emerge through an exercise of the will. But thanks to prudence, which is both an intellectual and an ethical virtue, they are inseparably bound to reason. "He alone can do good, who knows what things are like and what their situation is," says Pieper.[1]

The Judeo-Christian tradition brought a new element— heart—to the science of virtues: "When Holy Scripture refers to the heart," says Escrivá, "it does not refer to some fleeting sentiment of joy or tears. By heart it means the

---

1. J. Pieper, *Prudence.* p. 25.

personality which directs its whole being, body and soul, to what it considers its good, as Jesus Himself indicated: 'For where your treasure is, there will your heart be also.' . . . When we speak of a person's heart, we refer not just to his sentiments, but to the whole person." The heart is "the summary and source, expression and ultimate basis, of one's thoughts, words and actions. A man is worth what his heart is worth."[2]

Unlike the mind and the will, the heart is *not* an attribute of the human spirit. It is an expression signifying the whole person, the person himself: the heart does not just feel, it also knows and desires. Thus the intellect and the will come together in the heart.

"Our intelligence," says Jérôme Lejeune, "is not just an abstract machine; it is also incarnate, and the heart is as important as the faculty of reason, or more precisely, reason is nothing without the heart."[3] We need more than logic and scientific knowledge to practice prudence. "Reality," says Pieper, "is the prize solely of the highest form of cognition, and that is: seeing, intuition, contemplation."[4]

Prudence is sometimes called *wisdom of heart*. This means that love—the loftiest of passions—makes our intelligence more insightful so that we can better serve those we love.

Love may be blind, but, paradoxically, it also sharpens our vision, our capacity for moral insight. In the early 1990s, I met a U.S. diplomat who had worked for Ronald Reagan and was now directing the Moscow bureau of Radio Free Europe/Radio Liberty. He loved Russians so much—their

2. J. Escrivá, *Christ Is Passing By*, no. 164.

3. See C. Lejeune, *op. cit.*, p. 31.

4. J. Pieper, *Happiness and Contemplation*. South Bend, IN: Saint Augustine Press, 1998, p. 69.

culture and their way of being—that he was constantly generating new ideas on how to help Russia build its future.

By contrast, a participant in one of my *Virtuous Leadership* seminars, a European businessman who worked for a major company, told me that after five years in Russia he still didn't know "how to deal with these people." This top manager was a fine person, but because he didn't love Russians, his mind was unable to generate positive ideas on "how to deal with them."

The intellect is not a computer; it is incarnate, a thing rooted in the heart. Nor is the will a kind of turbo-charged reactor. Will power does not stem from self-discipline alone, but also from a moral sense rooted in the heart and giving rise to virtuous action: a *sense of good* stimulates prudence; a *sense of honor* stimulates courage; a *sense of shame* stimulates self-control; a *sense of compassion* stimulates justice; a *sense of beauty* stimulates magnanimity; a *sense of God* and man stimulates humility.

To live the virtues requires an exercise of will, but to achieve real excellence requires more than mere self-discipline. We must tend to our hearts, and to the seed of virtue planted there. The German philosopher Dietrich von Hildebrand speaks of allowing values to interpenetrate in the heart: "The inward nobility of good, its intrinsic beauty, touches the heart of the humble man and delights him."[5]

Leaders habitually contemplate that which is good and great and noble in the life of heroes, for the vision of the beautiful, as Plato says, causes the soul to sprout wings.[6]

"Whenever a ray of beauty, goodness, or holiness *wounds* our heart," writes Hildebrand, "whenever we abandon ourselves

---

5. D. von Hildebrand, *Transformation in Christ*. Ft. Collins, CO: Ignatius Press, 2001, p. 155.
6. Plato, *Phaedrus*. 249d.

in contemplative relaxation to a true value . . . that value may penetrate us wholly and elevate us above ourselves."[7]

We have all met people who, having come into contact with extraordinary goodness or beauty or sanctity, are impelled to make a radical response often entailing a thorough change of life, a kind of conversion. Ivan Lupandin, a Russian physicist who later became a professor of philosophy, once told me that after reading *One Day in the Life of Ivan Denisovich*, Aleksandr Solzhenitsyn's account of the travails of a simple peasant convict in a Siberian Gulag camp, he felt wounded by goodness, to paraphrase Hildebrand—the goodness of Ivan Denisovich, his creator, and his creator's moral vision. So powerful was the effect of Solzhenitsyn's writing that Lupandin felt morally compelled to make a clear choice between good and evil. He vividly recalls the day he changed his life by embracing good: June 26, 1975.

Father Guy Barbier, a leading figure of the Catholic Church in Finland and Estonia, was also "wounded" by goodness. He was 20 years old and still a layman when the Nazis arrested him in France and sent him to Leipzig to work in a munitions factory. Through clandestine channels, he contacted the French Resistance. The Gestapo intercepted his communications, arrested him, and sent him to a series of prisons and concentration camps, including Dachau and Buchenwald, over a period of six months. Finally, in a camp in Czechoslovakia, he fell grievously ill. His agony was so great that he was convinced he would die in camp. Two young Russian prisoners of war took it upon themselves to attend to him, doing so with utter selflessness and at considerable personal risk. Although his condition appeared hopeless, they nursed him back to health. Barbier never forgot

---

7. D. von Hildebrand, *op. cit.*, p. 231.

these two Russian prisoners: in their sacrifice he discovered his vocation to the priesthood.

A humble heart is virtue's point of departure. The humble person craves virtue. He must strengthen his will so as to turn his noble intentions into action, and he must not be afraid of human passions.

Leaders do not seek to excise passions from their personalities, but rather act in harmony with those they freely choose to cultivate.

The heart comprises not only values and moral sense, but also passions, which are natural components of the human psyche and are vital to our quest for personal excellence. People who suffer from severe emotional disorders or have a puritanical aversion to passion are at a serious disadvantage when it comes to achieving moral perfection.

Human passions contribute to the development of virtues when they positively interact with the *intellect* and the *will*. Through the intellect, leaders value those passions that contribute to the positive development of their personalities; through the will, they nurture those passions and bring them to bear in all their actions, even while giving no quarter to passions that are morally unworthy.

Only passions subsumed to the intellect and the will are authentic passions of the heart, of the whole person. Such passions become mature and stable impulses of the heart and contribute to our self-improvement. The *emotion* of love, for instance, becomes mature and stable only when it is based on a free and informed decision to love, understood as a freely chosen commitment to sacrifice for the sake of the loved one. Otherwise, it is likely to be a manifestation of physical attraction, which is here today, gone tomorrow.

Love should not be confused with sentimentality. The point of the former is commitment to another human being through thick and thin; the point of the latter is warm and fuzzy feelings as long as they last. The sentimentalist is willing to serve, but only as long as he gets an emotional kick from it.

The sentimentalist boss will often give his employees things they do not ask for and deny them what they really need. He will organize office parties for staff members to show his generosity, but will never correct them, because he fears he will *feel* bad about doing so. He personally cannot stand the thought of tension or confrontation. He is, in fact, a coward unable to serve his employees. Sentimentalism is false love.

Reason, will, and the heart blend seamlessly in the human person. We cannot separate one from the others without doing enormous damage to all three. Rationalists elevate the mind above all things, voluntarists the will, and sentimentalists the heart. Each approach corrupts them all, rendering people personally unhappy, professionally ineffective, and socially incompetent. Do not be deceived by their siren song. Insist on the anthropological unity of virtue, that is, on the unity of reason, will, and heart.

For reason, will and the heart enable us to do the three things vital to growing in virtue: 1) *contemplating* it so as to perceive its intrinsic beauty and desire it strongly (a matter of the heart); 2) *acting* virtuously habitually (a matter of the will) and 3) *practicing* all the virtues simultaneously with special attention given to prudence (a matter of reason.)

PART IV

LEADERSHIP AND SELF-FULFILLMENT

In Part Three we considered how leaders grow in virtues. Now we assess the *results* of our quest for virtue—human maturity and self-realization.

The leader's motive in striving for virtue is not simply to become good at what he does. Rather, it is to realize himself fully as a human being. Professional effectiveness is not the aim of self-improvement; it is merely one of its manifold (happy) results.

In this context, we will discover that *rules-based* ethics leave much to be desired and pale in comparison with the grandeur of *virtue* ethics.

CHAPTER 1

The Moral Profile of the Leader

> Maturity is the core of personal leadership: only
> a mature person is able to guide himself toward
> a freely chosen destiny as his personal mission.
>
> —*P. CARDONA AND P. GARCIA LOMBARDIA*

THROUGH THE VIRTUES WE ACHIEVE MATURITY in all its aspects—judgmental, emotional, and behavioral. Each has its own criteria. For example, we possess:

Maturity of judgment when we recognize our strengths and flaws, acknowledge our mission and social obligations, and eschew all fads, trends, and bromides;

Emotional maturity when we control our natural instincts, putting them at the service of our mission;

Behavioral maturity when our thoughts, judgments, and feelings are faithfully reflected in our actions. There is no question of leading a double life and no need for anyone to "figure us out."

The unmistakable signs of maturity are self-confidence and consistency, psychological stability, joy and optimism, naturalness, a sense of freedom and responsibility, and interior peace.

Leaders are mature, with a self-confidence born not of pride but of self-knowledge. They are consistent, which is not to say inflexible. In matters related to their mission, they know when to give ground and when to stand firm.

The immature person, by contrast, lacks self-confidence, because he lacks self-knowledge. He is unable to look at himself objectively. He exhibits childish pride or false humility. He is too prone to compromise, too ready to make demands. Imprudent, he charges recklessly ahead and indulges every whim. He cannot distinguish between what is important and what is not. His response to new realities is superficial or emotional. He avoids commitments and fears responsibilities. In fact, he fears himself and cannot find his place in society.

Immaturity often breeds *skepticism.* Many in their youth nurtured noble ambitions for personal leadership, dreaming of being strong, courageous, and selfless, of serving the whole of humanity. But because their values were not supported by virtues, they failed to overcome their personal weaknesses. Soon they renounced their dreams, became skeptical of human nature, and took refuge in material comfort, spiritual indifference, and self-indulgence.

Mature people, by contrast, know that by means of virtue they can overcome weakness and make their dreams come true. They know that human actualization is not achieved all at once, but step by step, taking into account the limitations proper to human nature. They are optimistic, positive, and patient with themselves and others.

Immaturity may lead to something worse than skepticism—namely, *cynicism,* or, the exaltation of human defects. A person convinced he cannot attain his moral objectives may sooner or later conclude that selfishness is not a vice but a virtue.

Leaders are neither skeptical nor cynical, but realistic. Realism is the ability to maintain the noblest aspirations of the soul even as one remains beset by personal weaknesses. This is not giving in to weaknesses, but transcending them through the practice of virtues.

King David, the leader of the Jewish people, is a good example of a man beset by personal weaknesses. Deeply flawed, he committed adultery and murder. But he converted, repented, and struggled to improve. He became a magnificent leader.

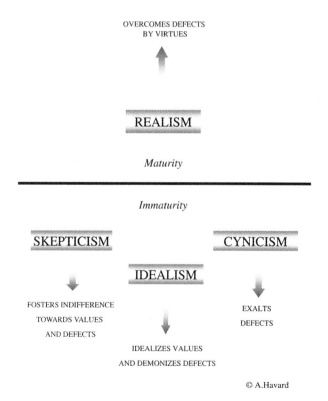

© A.Havard

Cynics and skeptics should never be trusted to lead others. They undermine morale and in this way compromise the mission of the organization.

Immature people should be kept as far from the levers of power as possible lest they harm the common good and, for that matter, themselves. Many people unconsciously assume, "What I *do* is not me; I am something else." Many politicians and businessmen fall into this trap. They do not appreciate the impact their decisions and actions have on their own interior lives. They fail to understand how much damage they do to themselves as human beings by living according to this false dichotomy between *doing* and *being*.

We have all heard the famous dictum, "Power corrupts; absolute power corrupts absolutely." But power makes virtuous people grow, which is why power should be in the hands of the virtuous. Power did not corrupt Thomas More. Precisely through the exercise of power, Thomas More became *Saint* Thomas More.

© A.Havard

CHAPTER 2

Virtue and Self-fulfillment

> Virtue is *ultimum potentiae*, the most a man "can be" of himself.
>
> — *THOMAS AQUINAS*

VIRTUE IS THE ENHANCEMENT of the human person in ways appropriate to his nature. To be virtuous means "to be your true self." Two thousand five hundred years ago the poet Pindar put it this way: "Become what you are."[1]

People who are hell-bent on self-fulfillment and yet fail to cultivate virtue tend to become slaves to fashion and the latest thing. Only through the practice of virtue can we flourish. Anything that leads us away from virtue alienates us from our very selves.

Leaders attain joy in practicing virtue. Immature people, by contrast, know nothing of this joy. They cannot even imagine it, because virtue for them is *terra incognita*.

The joy that comes from virtue is not smug. "Virtue," says Pieper, "is not the tame 'respectability' and 'uprightness' of the philistine."[2] Leaders are not interested in virtue as a

---

1. Pindar, *Pythian Ode*, II, 72.
2. J. Pieper, *On Hope*, chapt. 2 in J. Pieper, *Faith. Hope. Love.* p. 99.

kind of guarantee of moral superiority. They are interested in the good for its own sake.

Leaders are filled with joy not only when they practice virtue, but also when they see others doing the same. This feeling is an expression of the very real solidarity that unites all men of good will who seek the common good. We rejoice in the virtues of others because they show we are not alone in our quest for excellence.

It is *joy* that virtue confers, not *happiness*. Happiness is the eternal contemplation of God, which is the ultimate goal of life and exceeds our powers. There is nothing we can do to make ourselves happy. Happiness is a gift. Pieper says: "Man as he is constituted, endowed as he is with a thirst for happiness, cannot have his thirst quenched in the finite realm; and if he thinks or behaves as if that were possible, he is misunderstanding himself, he is acting contrary to his own nature."[3]

Although virtue does not *confer* happiness, it does bring us closer to attaining it because it brings us closer to God, who is Truth, Goodness, and Beauty. This will not happen if our hearts are set on money, power, fame, or sensuality. If they are, we will achieve not happiness, but alienation. The Russian writer Anton Chekhov depicts this sorry state in a short story. It concerns Nikolai Ivanovich and his dream of owning a *dacha* surrounded by gooseberry bushes. Having spent years scraping together the necessary funds, he finally realizes his dream and buys the *dacha*. To celebrate, he invites friends over to tea and serves them his precious gooseberries. The narrator—his brother—comments:

> "In the evening, while we were having tea, the cook laid a
> plateful of gooseberries on the table. They had not been

---

3. J. Pieper, *Happiness and Contemplation*. pp. 38–39.

bought, but were his own gooseberries, plucked for the first time since the bushes were planted. Nikolai Ivanovich laughed with joy and for a minute or two he looked in silence at the gooseberries with tears in his eyes. He could not speak for excitement, then put one into his mouth, glanced at me in triumph, like a child at last being given its favorite toy, and said:

'How good they are!'

He went on eating greedily, and saying all the while:

'How good they are! Do try one!'

It was hard and sour, but, as Pushkin said, the illusion, which exalts us, is dearer to us than ten thousand truths. I saw a happy man, one whose dearest dream had come true, who had attained his goal in life, who had got what he wanted, and was pleased with his destiny and with himself. In my idea of human life there is always some alloy of sadness, but now at the sight of a happy man I was filled with something like despair."[4]

Nikolai Ivanovich deceives himself in thinking that material things lead to happiness. He is so deluded that he finds the sour, unripe gooseberries delicious. He is alienated from truth and reality, and therefore from himself. Such alienation is typical of the immature.

---

4. A. Chekhov, *Gooseberries*. New York: Charles Scribner's Sons, 1917.

CHAPTER 3

The Pitfalls of Rules-based Ethics

Who rejects evil not because it is forbidden, but because it is evil, is truly free.

—*ROBERT SPAEMANN*

THERE ARE TWO KINDS OF ETHICS: rules-based ethics and virtue ethics. The former, as the name implies, is grounded in law: an action is *correct* if it conforms to the law, *incorrect* if it does not; the latter is grounded in human nature: *good* is that which brings us closer to moral perfection, *bad* that which leads us away from it.

Virtue ethics does not deny the validity of laws, but it does insist that laws cannot be the ultimate foundation of ethics. Laws must be at the service of virtue. That is the proper order of things.

The Ten Commandments, taken at face value, appear to be an exercise in rules-based ethics, *par excellence*: Thou shalt not steal, thou shalt not kill, thou shalt not commit adultery, etc. Here, God reveals his will in the form of laws, which we submit to or not. To fail to submit is to sin.

In *virtue ethics*, God also reveals his will, but now as a positive affirmation of human selfhood. To violate this law is to do more than sin. It is to harm oneself.

Ultimately, the Ten Commandments *serve* virtue, and in so doing transcend themselves becoming much more than a series of negative moral prohibitions: "Thou shalt not steal," understood in the light of virtue, becomes: "Practice detachment in relation to the things of this world." "Thou shalt not kill" becomes: "Cherish life and respect it always." "Thou shalt not commit adultery" becomes: "Be pure of heart and mind and body and soul."

Jesus Christ is the supreme interpreter of the Old Covenant, including the Ten Commandments. He repeatedly links its prohibitions to positive virtues and makes it clear that God the Father wills the moral perfection of each one of us.

For Christians, any failure to observe the Ten Commandments is a sin, as *is any act in contradiction of the virtues.*

I will not grow in virtue if I do not obey the Commandments. If I worship sex, money, and power, if I blithely trash the reputation of others, if I fail to honor my parents, in short, if I fly in the face of the Commandments, I am on a slippery slope to personal disintegration.

And yet if I am intent on personal excellence, I must do more than observe the letter of the Commandments. I must cultivate and live by the virtues to which the Commandments point.

"The law acts from outside," says the German philosopher Robert Spaemann. "After it has helped us understand what is good and what is evil, and after it has given rise to a habit, the virtue itself becomes the rule. He who rejects evil not because it is forbidden, but because it is evil, is truly free."[1]

---

1. R. Spaemann, *Main Concepts of Morals.* München: Moralische Grundbegriffe, Beck'sche Verlagsbuchhandlung, 1986. See chapter "Freedom and Moral Obligation."

How leaders behave is determined less by the law than by their virtues. If, for example, leaders do not slander their competitors, that is not so much because slander is forbidden by both moral and criminal law, as because people of character would not stoop so low in the first place. It simply would not occur to them.

The concept of work ethics—the ethical codes that govern the world of work—has much to do with rules and little with virtue.

Work ethics indeed are limited to external, visible actions I perform on the job, and to the ethical rules of my profession and the enterprise I work for. Work ethics aim at professional rectitude, not human perfection.

Of course, since this rectitude contributes to the respectability of the enterprise and those who work for it, it is a good thing. But it is not enough. I can scrupulously observe these norms yet stagnate as a human being. That happens when I confuse human excellence with mere observance of a code. It is possible to fulfill exterior ethical norms without having a clue about how they relate to my personality. Work ethics is a starting point, not a goal. By itself, it does not lead to personal improvement.

Professional rectitude is good and necessary, but, unless reinforced by virtues, it runs the risk of ringing false, and thereby possibly undermining the credibility of the organization.

Many organizations maintain codes of conduct that enshrine their corporate ethics. But if the people in those organizations do not habitually practice the human virtues, codes of conduct, no matter how high-minded, can become so much window-dressing.

Another drawback of work ethics is implied in its name. It may lead some to believe that there are two kinds of ethics, one for work and another for off-hours. Some people are vigilant about maintaining a strict code of conduct at work, but regard private life as another matter: "What I do on my own time is my business." All too often, they misuse the gift of time by using off hours to "kick back" and indulge their whims and fantasies. They believe working hard entitles them to this indulgence, which they elevate to the status of a right. Others are capable of more egregious behavior such as drinking excessively, two-timing their wives, or showing not the slightest concern in their treatment of another human being. Yet they are absolutely certain that they are ethical people because they observe a corporate code of conduct, behave in a generally professional manner, and pay their bills. They lead a double life.

Leaders, by contrast, behave virtuously always and everywhere: at work, with the family, among friends, during free time, and even when they are alone. This is because they live by virtue ethics, which unify one's personality and daily activities, both public and private, thereby making the living of a double life impossible.

Rules work best for children, who need to know precisely where they stand, what is acceptable behavior and what is not. As soon as they reach the age of reason, however, they must be taught the "why" of rules, so as to grasp their connection with human nature and human perfection.

Rules leave much to be desired for adults. They fail to satisfy a mature person's intelligence and are too narrow in scope to cover the variety of life situations people typically encounter. Virtues are needed more than rules. If I possess prudence, I will not be at a loss upon finding myself in uncharted waters. I will know how to make the right choices.

Rules-based ethics tends to be self-referential. Rules are rarely thought of as linked to the human quest for moral perfection (although they are). This makes them curiously fragile, often ineffective, and sometimes dangerous. They can easily be tossed aside and replaced by ideology, pragmatic objectives, esoteric spirituality, vacuous and trendy notions . . . or whatever. How many Communist officials in Central and Eastern Europe became instant liberal democrats after the fall of the Berlin Wall? It was a simple matter to exchange one set of rules for another.

The West today is largely a rules-based culture. Vast numbers of people play by the rules. For them the demands of career and professional success are the supreme rule, the only valid point of reference for their everyday behavior. The ideal of sainthood has been widely replaced by the ideal of having a big, glamorous career, no matter what must be done to achieve it.

By contrast, a person who seeks after virtue will not easily surrender to ideologies or fashion. Having interiorized the unchanging principles of human nature, he has achieved a spiritual solidity that renders him impervious to the siren song of a debased mass culture.

Rules-based ethics tends to produce narrow, unimaginative people little given to reflection on deeper meanings.

A friend of mine told me the following story: "I was interested in swimming regularly at the local swimming pool, so I signed up for a plan that was cheap. It included both swimming and weightlifting. I wasn't interested in the latter, but I bought the membership anyway because the price was right. After a few weeks it was brought to my attention that I hadn't been lifting weights. The woman at the counter said this was unacceptable because weightlifting was part of the membership plan. I asked why management should care as long I paid my dues. She said I had no right to swim without first lifting weights because 'that is the rule.' I asked her to explain the purpose behind this rule, but all she could do was invoke the rulebook. It was like talking to a brick wall. She threatened me with expulsion if I did not work out with weights for at least 15 minutes before hitting the pool."

Someone obsessed with observing rules does not study problems in depth, investigate concrete circumstances, or take the initiative. He makes decisions, but he does not really deliberate. Creativity is not his strong suit.

How different it is for those engaged in the quest for moral perfection! No pre-cooked solutions for them. Virtue is always original, creative, and multi-faceted.

PART V

TOWARDS VICTORY

Having spoken of the role of *natural* virtues in leadership, we now turn our attention to the *supernatural* virtues of faith, hope, and charity. In doing so, we will refer to theological concepts not encountered previously in this book.

This shift in emphasis may be jarring for some readers, especially those who do not share the Christian faith. They may be content to live by the purely human virtues. If so, and if they sincerely seek the truth, they will still become outstanding leaders in their fields, and, what is more, will lead lives hugely pleasing to God. That is because neither the human virtues nor the theological virtues are inventions of men; they are expressions of the goodness of God.

Still, leaders who cultivate faith, hope, and charity do have a decided advantage in their quest for excellence. No study of the impact of virtue on leadership is complete without them.

In the final chapter, we set forth a methodology for interior growth tailored to the needs of busy, professional people. It will be expressed in terms most readily comprehensible by Christians but adaptable to non-Christian ways of thinking and being.

CHAPTER 1

The Impact of Christian Life

> . . . you and I and everyone may be sure that nothing perfects our personality so much as correspondence with grace.
>
> —*JOSEMARÍA ESCRIVÁ*, FURROW, *NO. 443*

NATURAL VIRTUES ARE UNIVERSALLY VALID. The Greeks, the Chinese, the Japanese, the Romans, and the Jews of olden times all embraced the human virtues. In fact, there is no national culture that does not recognize their high value in one way or another.

The *Book of Wisdom*, written some 150 years before Christ, declares: "Wisdom teaches self-control and prudence, justice and courage, and nothing in life is more useful than these."[1] This Old Testament reference to the four cardinal virtues shows that the Jewish author of the inspired text drank deeply of the wisdom of the ancient Greeks.

It is Christianity, however, that sets the greatest store by the human virtues. Jesus Christ, the Incarnate Son of God, is

---

1. Wis 8:7.

perfect God and perfect Man. Christ's humanity was not absorbed or suppressed by his Divinity. On the contrary, He practiced the *human* virtues to perfection.

The challenge for Christian leaders—and it is a vast one—is to "attain . . . to mature manhood, to the measure of the stature of the fullness of Christ."[2] Christian leaders do this by striving to make their own the virtues, both human and divine, of their Master. They attain maturity and strength from the synergy between the natural virtues, *acquired* by their own efforts, and the supernatural ones, *infused* by God in their souls.

Before exploring the relationship between natural and supernatural virtues, let us first consider the Christian leader's privileged position.

THE CHRISTIAN LEADER'S PRIVILEGED POSITION

Leaders, no matter what their religious or philosophical convictions are, feel the promptings of the natural moral law, compelling them to do good and avoid evil. Leaders are, of course, as subject to sinful inclinations as anyone else. But they know that if they habitually practice virtue, they will strengthen their character and overcome their flaws.

Thanks to Old Testament revelation, Jewish and Christian leaders are wiser than even the wisest of classical philosophers. They know that natural moral law comes from the Creator who inscribes it in every human heart. They know that their inclination towards evil is the bitter fruit of *Original Sin*, which all of mankind mysteriously inherited by means of natural generation.

---

2. Eph 4:13.

Christian leaders know through the New Testament and Church Tradition that, at Baptism, the Holy Spirit infuses into their souls a precious supernatural gift, consisting of three elements—sanctifying grace,* the theological virtues of faith, hope, and charity,** and the seven gifts of the Holy Spirit.*** Mortal sin can cause us to forfeit these supernatural habits, but we can earn them back through the sacrament of Confession.

They also know it is the will of Christ that we, in His words, "be perfect, as your heavenly Father is perfect."[3] They take to heart the words of Saint Paul: "This is the will of God—your sanctification."[4] The struggle for perfection finds its highest justification and motivation in Christianity: the achievement of sanctity, which is both a natural and a supernatural process, is the will of God for all of us.

Christian leaders have a model of human and divine perfection—Jesus Christ. Mary, His Immaculate Mother, emulates her Son so faithfully and patterns every aspect of her being on Him so closely, that Dante calls her, in a striking

---

* Sanctifying grace is an *ontological* supernatural habit that heals the soul of sin and elevates it to enable it to live with God (see *Catechism of the Catholic Church* [*CCC*], 1999 and 2000).

** Faith, hope, and charity are called the theological virtues, for they relate directly to God (through faith I believe in God and believe all that He has said; through hope I desire eternal life and rely on the help of God in order to attain it; through charity I love God above all things for His own sake, and my neighbors for the love of God). The theological virtues are *operative* supernatural habits, which dispose us to choose and act in ways proper to the children of God. They are the foundation of Christian moral activity; they animate it and give it its special character. They inform and give life to all the other virtues (*CCC*, 1812–1813).

*** The seven gifts of the Holy Spirit are wisdom, understanding, counsel, fortitude, knowledge, piety, and fear of the Lord (see Is 11:1–2). These are *operative* supernatural habits, which make Christians docile in following the promptings of the Holy Spirit (*CCC*, 1830).

3. Mt 5:48.

4. 1 Thess 4:3.

phrase, "the daughter of her Son." Mary's single-mindedness in emulating Jesus makes her a model for all Christians in all seasons.

If to lead is to serve others even to the nth degree, then Christ's sacrifice of His life on Calvary for our sakes, which is renewed in each and every celebration of the Holy Eucharist, must constitute any leader's supreme inspiration. Indeed, through the Holy Eucharist leaders grow in their spirit of service.

Leaders rely in a special way on prayer. Karl von Habsburg, Emperor of Austria-Hungary, never made important decisions without first "praying it," as he used to say, meaning discussing the matter with God. Stolypin, Schuman, Lejeune, and Reagan all prayed.

When asked in a 1993 interview which of her leadership practices she would like to see continued after stepping down as president of the Philippines, Cory Aquino replied without hesitation, "The habit of prayer. . . . The great of the world should pray, if only for the sake of those who must endure their greater capacity for tragic errors."[5]

In prayer, leaders acquire the light to decide prudently and the energy to act courageously. Stolypin, sensing he was likely to be killed for his beliefs (as indeed he was), said, "I offer up a prayer every morning and think of the day ahead as my last. . . . In the evening, I thank God for granting me one more day of life."[6]

In prayer, leaders learn to interpret the signs sent to them by God's Providence: "I had learned in my years of imprisonment," writes Aleksandr Solzhenitsyn, "to sense that guiding hand, to glimpse that bright meaning beyond

---

5. C. Aquino, *op. cit.*
6. See S. Rybas, *Stolypin*. Moscow: Molodaya Gvardia, 2004, p. 226.

and above my self and my wishes. I had not always been quick to understand the sudden upsets in my life, and often, out of bodily and spiritual weakness, had seen in them the very opposite of their true meaning and their far-off purpose. Later the true significance of what had happened would inevitably become clear to me and I would become numb with surprise. I have done many things in my life that conflicted with the great aims I had set myself—and something has always set me on the true path again. I have become so used to this, come to rely on it so much, that the only task I need set myself is to interpret as clearly and quickly as I can each major event in my life."[7]

In prayer leaders purify their motives, affirm their values, and contemplate Christ, whose life they see as intimately bound up with their own. In Him they discover their destiny and vocation, and develop a deeper awareness of their strengths and weaknesses.

Thus, the Christian leader has a unique advantage—he knows he has a vocation to holiness, a model to follow (Christ), and, at his disposal, the invincible means of prayer and the sacraments, through which he receives the supernatural virtues of faith, hope, and charity.

THE HUMAN FOUNDATIONS OF CHRISTIAN LEADERSHIP

Christian leaders are not content with merely natural perfection. They have their sights set on the loftiest conceivable goal—holiness. Nothing less will do. To achieve their objective, they must have frequent recourse to the supernatural virtues of faith, hope, and charity.

---

7. Aleksandr Solzhenitsyn, *The Oak and the Calf.* p. 111.

But this does not mean giving short shrift to the natural virtues. The natural virtues constitute the very foundation of the supernatural ones. If I make no effort to cultivate magnanimity or prudence, the theological virtues of faith, hope, and charity will not intervene to make me magnanimous or prudent in spite of myself. If I give in to cowardice, intemperance, or egoism, I cannot expect the theological virtues to step into the fray and make me courageous, temperate, and just.

No amount of religious observance can compensate for the failure to practice natural virtue.

"There are many Christians," writes Escrivá, "who follow Christ and are astonished by His divinity, but forget Him as a Man. And they fail in the practice of supernatural virtues, despite all the external paraphernalia of piety, because they do nothing to acquire human virtues."[8]

This insistence on the supreme importance of the human virtues was central to Escrivá's teaching. He once wrote: "If we accept the responsibility of being children of God, we will realize that God wants us to be very human. Our heads should indeed be touching heaven, but our feet should be firmly planted on the ground. The price of living as Christians is not one of ceasing to be human or of abandoning the effort to acquire the natural virtues, which some people have even without knowing Christ. The price paid for each Christian is the redeeming Blood of our Lord and He, I insist, wants us to be both very human and very divine, struggling each day to imitate Him who is *perfectus Deus, perfectus homo*."[9]

---

8. J. Escrivá, *Furrow*, no. 652.

9. J. Escrivá, *Friends of God*, no. 75.

THE IMPACT OF SUPERNATURAL VIRTUE

The natural virtues constitute the foundation of the supernatural ones, even as the latter strengthen us in the practice of the former, raising it to a higher level.

Leaders cannot achieve *natural perfection* without the help of divine grace. So profound is the disorder provoked by Original Sin that without divine grace they would never succeed in their quest for perfection no matter how many virtues and talents they possessed. Only grace infused into the soul heals man's wounded nature and gives him any possibility of attaining ultimate personal excellence.

There is a stage beyond ordinary *natural* perfection, however. It is called *Christian* perfection. Natural perfection calls for the practice of the natural virtues proper to *human beings*, while Christian perfection entails *also* the practice of the supernatural virtues of faith, hope, and charity proper to *children* of God.

Faith, hope, and charity build upon and shape the human virtues, including prudence. The supernatural virtues elevate, strengthen, and transfigure the natural ones.

Here are some considerations (by no means exhaustive) on how theological virtues interact with and enrich purely human virtues.

Christian magnanimity, which is natural magnanimity informed by faith, hope, and charity, expands the heart of the Christian leader, enabling him to respond generously to his vocation. His aspiration towards great things, the hallmark of his youth, continues to flourish as he grows in supernatural maturity. As the psalm puts it, he finds his "youth is renewed like the eagle's."[10]

---

10. Psalm 103 (102):5; Liturgy of St. John Chrysostom, Antiphon 1.

There's a lot to be said for Christian magnanimity. For one thing, Europe as we know it might never have come into being but for the magnanimity of a sixth-century Italian monk called Benedict. Born in a time and place beset by corruption, and, after the fall of the Western Roman Empire, repeated barbarian invasions, Benedict saw the challenge facing Europe as essentially spiritual and cultural. He and his followers, who came to be known as Benedictines, established a network of monastic communities across Europe, eventually numbering 80 in Benedict's own lifetime. These communities were repositories of Christian faith and the inherited culture, islands in the torrent of barbarism sweeping across the continent. They were largely responsible for the preservation of Western civilization.

In the East, Saints Cyril and Methodius, Greek monks and blood brothers born in ninth-century Thessalonica, displayed a magnanimity that paralleled Saint Benedict's in the West. With the support of various bishops of Rome and patriarchs of Constantinople, they conceived a bold vision for bringing the pagan, Slavic tribes of Europe into the Christian communion by devising a Greek-based alphabet to enable them to read the New Testament and the Church Fathers in their own language. This became know as Cyrillic, in honor of Saint Cyril.

The holy Greek brothers faced slander, torture and abuse as they went about laying the foundations of Slavic culture and thereby fostering the spiritual flowering of the continent. "By exercising their own charism," wrote Pope John Paul II, "Cyril and Methodius made a decisive contribution to the building of Europe not only in Christian religious communion but also to its civil and cultural union."[11]

---

11. See John Paul II, *Slavorum apostoli*. 27.

In the centuries since then, women and men like Catherine of Siena and Joan of Arc, Francis of Assisi, Dominic and Sergei of Radonezh,* Teresa of Avila, John of the Cross, Bridget of Sweden, Ignatius of Loyola, and Mother Teresa of Calcutta have been heroic figures. But they also have been something more: magnanimous dreamers with a powerful sense of mission.

Christian magnanimity is deeply rooted in the theological virtue of hope, which causes us to trust in God. Saint Josemaría Escrivá was a great exponent of hope. This is apparent in a written account of a meeting he had with members of the women's section of Opus Dei in 1942 in Madrid.

He opened the meeting by sketching a series of ambitious projects aimed at promoting human and spiritual development and alleviating poverty around the world. The idea was that the women's section would manage these projects—even though it had only three members, all of them living in a Madrid still devastated by the effects of the Spanish Civil War.

Encarnita Ortega wrote: "On the desk, [Father Josemaría] placed a chart showing the different projects that the women's branch of Opus Dei was going to carry out in the world. Just trying to follow the Father almost made me dizzy, he was explaining them all to us so vividly: agricultural schools for rural women, professional training schools, university residences, maternity homes in cities all over the world, book-mobiles bringing wholesome and educational

---

* Monk, spiritual father to countless souls and master of the interior life, Sergei of Radonezh (1322–1392) was one of the brilliant lights of Russian Orthodoxy. In 1334, he established Trinity monastery in the dense woods of Central Russia near the town of Radonezh, some fifty kilometers from Moscow. By virtue of his hard work, constant prayer, and great sanctity, Trinity monastery would become Russia's principal center of Orthodox religious life. Now called Trinity-Saint Sergei in honor of its holy founder, it remains so to this day.

reading to the most remote villages, bookstores. . . . Slowly folding up that chart, he said: 'There are two possible reactions to all this. One is to think it's very nice, but an impossible dream. The other is to trust in the Lord, to trust that if he asks this of us, he will help us make it a reality. I hope you react the second way.' But the reality then and there was hunger and fatigue, scarcity and poverty."[12]

Conditions in Spain in 1942 were by no means auspicious for the realization of such ambitious dreams. But Escrivá was filled with and driven by supernatural hope. In succeeding years, all the projects he envisioned in 1942 came to fruition.

Christian magnanimity is reinforced by the gift of knowledge—one of the seven gifts of the Holy Spirit. Knowledge allows the Christian leader to perceive the limits of relying purely on human means and to rely more and more on God's assistance. Here is a letter written by Pyotr Stolypin to his wife Olga, on April 26, 1906, after learning that the Tsar had appointed him Minister of Internal Affairs, a position that put him directly in the firing line of anti-government terrorists: "Olga, my priceless treasure. Yesterday, my fate was decided. I am the Minister of Internal Affairs of a bloody, battered country representing one-sixth of the earth's surface, and this at one of the most difficult periods in history, of the kind that recurs once in a thousand years [ed., two of Stolypin's recent predecessors had been assassinated]. Human strength counts for little; what is needed is deep faith in God, strong hope that He supports and instructs me. Lord, help me. I feel that He will not abandon me; I feel a serenity which will not desert me."[13]

---

12. A. Vasquez de Prada, *op. cit.*, vol. 2, p. 400.
13. S. Rybas, *op. cit.*, p. 60.

Informed by the theological virtue of faith, humility—the habit of living in the truth—attains cosmic importance for the Christian leader. It allows him to grasp the deepest truth about himself, the truth that he is a child of God, not just a creature of God. This awareness of his divine sonship is, for the Christian leader, an enormous stimulus to magnanimity: If I am a son of God, then I must dream God's dreams.

And when humility—the habit of service—comes to be informed by the theological virtue of charity, there is another transcendent effect: the Christian leader is stimulated to serve God and man unconditionally.

When informed by faith, hope, and charity, prudence—the quintessential virtue of decision-makers—enables the Christian leader to judge situations from a perspective akin to God's. Christian prudence is reinforced by the gifts of wisdom, understanding, and counsel.

Courage informed by charity and strengthened by the gift of fortitude enables the Christian leader to apply his principles consistently in all circumstances, starting with himself.

Courage, when informed by charity, can give the Christian leader the ability to endure extraordinary suffering. The story of Dr. Takashi Nagai of Nagasaki, a Japanese scientist and Catholic convert from atheism, is a case in point.

On August 9, 1945, the day the atomic bomb was dropped on Nagasaki, Nagai was working in the radiology department of the Nagasaki University hospital. He suffered immediate effects from the blast—hardly surprising, as his office was located just 700 yards from the epicenter. Thrown to the ground while filing x-rays in his office, Nagai sustained severe lacerations in the side from flying glass. His beloved wife, Midori, was not so lucky—he found her carbonized remains in what was left of their home. Despite his grief and his serious physical injuries, Nagai volunteered for relief efforts and worked tirelessly for several months treating the seemingly endless stream of atomic-bomb victims.

Bedridden by the spring of 1947 (he had contracted leukemia working as a radiologist during the war), he nevertheless resolved to use the time remaining to him, and the parts of his body that still functioned (hands, head, heart) to promote a durable peace among nations through charity. He wrote and published extensively on this theme in the last years of life, moving many souls to contemplate his Christian message.[14]

Known as the Saint of Nagasaki, he became world-renowned for the peace he exuded. People flocked to see him from all corners of Japan, Emperor Hirohito among them. Pope Pius XII wrote him and sent him gifts. More than 20,000 people attended his funeral in 1951 as the bells of Buddhist temples, Shinto shrines, and Christian churches rang out across Japan.

Informed by the theological virtue of charity, temperance takes on a transcendent new meaning: We must respect our body because it is the temple of the Holy Spirit; we must do penance and fast so as to atone for our sins; we must direct our passions to the service of God. Christian temperance is reinforced by the *gift of filial fear*—fear of losing the indwelling of the Holy Trinity in our soul.

Justice, informed by the supernatural virtue of charity, inspires the Christian leader to treat everyone with love and mercy, for each person is created in the image of God and called to eternal life. Christian justice is reinforced by the *gift of*

---

14. See P. Glynn, *A Song for Nagasaki*. Grand Rapids, MI: Eerdmans Publishers, Co., 1990.

piety, which helps the Christian leader to fulfill his duties towards God, family, country, and indeed all of humanity.

Supernatural maturity promotes natural maturity. There are many examples of young people who have shown unexpected maturity thanks to their practice of faith, hope, and charity. A notable case in point is Saint Joan of Arc, the Maid of Orleans. This illiterate, 19-year-old girl withstood interrogation by a kangaroo court and its terrifying, cynical presiding officer. The wisdom and simplicity of her rebuttals to the unjust accusations leveled against her remain astonishing 500 years later. When the tribunal accused her of having disobeyed her parents by leaving home and embarking on her mission without their consent, Joan gave a magnificent lesson in basic theology: "Were I to have one hundred fathers and one hundred mothers, and were I the daughter of a King, I would have gone because God commanded it."

In the liturgy of the Mass of St. Joan of Arc, the first reading is from the *Book of Wisdom*: "Through Wisdom I shall have glory among the multitudes and honor in the presence of the elders, though I am young. I shall be found keen in judgment, and in the sight of rulers I shall be admired. When I am silent they will wait for me, and when I speak they will give heed; and when I speak at greater length they will put their hands on their mouths."[15]

Another example of supernatural maturity aiding and abetting natural maturity is Vanya Moiseyev, a Baptist believer who was tortured and killed by the Soviet KGB in 1972 while serving in the Red Army. The KGB targeted Vanya for no other reason than that he was a Christian believer.

---

15. Wis 8:10.

On June 15, he wrote to his parents:

"The Lord has shown me the way and I must follow it. And I have decided to do so. But I do not know if I will return alive because the combat is harder than before. I face a struggle more severe than the one that preceded it, although I am not afraid; Jesus walks before me. May my beloved parents not be sad: It is because I love Jesus more than myself that I obey him, although the body is fearful of all it must endure. But I do not value life as much as I love Jesus. And I would not expect things to turn out according to my will, but as the Lord wishes it. He will say go and I will go."

On July 16 he died, having succumbed to torture. He had courageously refused the KGB what it sought—the renunciation of his faith. He was 20 years old.[16]

Here is an example of a teenager who died an untimely death in 1985, but only after achieving remarkable maturity. Alexia Gonzalez-Barros, a Spanish girl, was stricken by cancer at a young age. She accepted her illness with joy and offered it to God for specific intentions. Her constant prayer was, "Jesus, may I always do your will." She had to wear a large metallic brace affixed to her head and neck with screws, and was given medicine that turned her mouth a dark, unattractive color. Despite everything, she kept her cheerfulness and good humor throughout. She said to her friends, "First, they made me look like Frankenstein; now, I look more like Dracula!" She always steered conversation toward her visitors and away from herself. When her doctor

---

16. See D. Rance, "Ivan Moissev: Le martyre d'un jeune apôtre moldave," in *Martyrs Chrétiens d' URSS*. Bibliotèque AED, Collection "Témoins" 2002, p. 387; M. Grant, *Vanya: A True Story, Chester*. UK: Creation House Press, 1995; P. M. Vincenti Guzzi, *Vanja e gli Angeli*, Rome, 1994.

brought medical students to observe her, he told them, "I want you to see how it is to be joyful, despite pain and suffering." Alexia died, transfigured by the grace of God, at the age of 14.[17]

Some might say saints are not good role models because their standards are too high for mere mortals like the rest of us. But saints are mortals, too. They simply are determined to achieve moral perfection, and it is that which makes them saints. It also is what makes the difference between a leader and an also-ran.

Exponents of secular materialism such as Nietzsche taught that the Gospels stifle human nature. History is replete with examples that prove the contrary. In our own times, a multitude of Christian leaders has come forward to light up the world with their love of Christ. Some were priests or religious—Pope John Paul II, Saint Josemaría Escrivá, Mother Teresa of Calcutta, to name a few. Others were lay people: Pyotr Stolypin, Robert Schuman, Aleksandr Solzhenitsyn, and Jérôme Lejeune, among others. All blazed a trail for those who would come after them.

But what of Nietzsche's vaunted "superman," who, sufficient to himself, had no need of God? His monuments are Auschwitz and Kolyma.

---

17. See M. Monge, *Alexia: A Story of Joy and Heroism in Suffering.* Manila: Sinag-Tala, 1994.

CHAPTER 2

An Agenda for Victory

Achieving Personal Excellence

> Your greatest enemy is your own self.
>
> —JOSEMARÍA ESCRIVÁ, THE WAY, NO. 225

THE ESSENCE OF LEADERSHIP IS CHARACTER, and the essence of character is the lifelong quest for personal excellence. Striving to live the virtues, we do what God wants us to do. The way may be strewn with obstacles, but we will prevail. God does not set us up for failure.

This chapter examines the concrete steps to make meaningful progress in living the virtues. These include:

1. A method for assessing one's own behavior, values, and priorities—i.e., *examination of conscience.*
2. Guidance from a qualified *spiritual director.*
3. Devising and conscientiously living a "*plan of life.*"

While this program is expressed here in terms that derive from Christian faith, all great religions embrace the human virtues and have spiritual practices and devotions that foster interior growth.

Before exploring these points in depth, however, let's look at some of the main stumbling blocks.

THE OBSTACLES:

1. *Moral conformism.* Be prepared to swim against the powerful currents of egoism, relativism, and material- ism today sweeping the world. Pay no attention to what others say. Turn a deaf ear and a blind eye to all trends, in whatever sphere, that lack the ring of truth. Glory in your counter-cultural stance. You will stand out as a beacon of truth.

2. *Perfectionism.* Perfectionism has little to do with love for perfection. It means that we do not accept failure—and when failure comes, we feel humiliated and abandon the struggle. Perfectionism comes from pride.

   Chances are good we will fail at some point in our quest. The danger then is that those of us who are per- fectionists will give up and give in to mediocrity.

   We have to be like sportsmen who begin again after each failure. We need the simplicity and resilience of chil- dren, who, having stumbled, bounce back like rubber balls. We must see every day—every hour—as a new chapter in our life, as indeed it is.

3. *Impatience.* Virtue, like wine, matures slowly. Do not force the issue. Be at peace. Sudden changes can and do take place in religious and philosophical convictions, but are rare, indeed scarcely conceivable, where charac- ter is concerned. Give it time.

4. *Garden-variety obliviousness.* Because we persist in thinking that matters of the spirit are divorced from temporal affairs, we fail to realize that the people next to us—spouses and children, clients and colleagues—are collaborators, however unwitting, in our noble quest for personal excellence (and we in theirs). Escrivá says: "Without that friction produced by contact with others, how would you ever lose those corners, those edges and projections—the imperfections and defects—of your character, and acquire the smooth and regular finish, the firm flexibility of charity, of perfection?"[1]

We should see even people we're not particularly fond of as gifts rather than nuisances. Without realizing it, they provide us with countless occasions to be better. We need prudence to determine the best way to deal with them, self-control not to get angry, courage to be patient, and justice to give them their due despite everything. In many cases, this would mean helping them identify their flaws and improve their characters.

5. *The tendency to go easy on oneself.* This natural tendency can seriously impede, if not derail, your quest. Take control of your *self.* Put aside your moods, and whims, your base desires, and precious opinions. Raise the level of your spiritual game. Ascend to the heights, then never come down.

But how? How can I overcome the obstacles to victory, including the greatest obstacle of all . . . my own self? As follows.

---

1. J. Escrivá, *The Way*, no. 20.

EXAMINATION OF CONSCIENCE

Spend three minutes at the end of each day reviewing how you lived the virtues that day. Resolve to root out unworthy attitudes and forms of behavior at once. Follow these pointers:

A. *Keep in mind the aim of the exam.* You are seeking insight into where you stand in your daily quest for personal excellence. It has nothing to do with psychoanalysis or navel gazing.

   If done persistently and well, it should give rise to sincere contrition and a sincere change of heart.

   It is future-oriented because it impels you to improve tomorrow what you failed to do well today. The exam is intended to weed out your vices and defects so that you remain in top spiritual condition for pursuing your quest.

B. *Distinguish well between defects of character and defects of temperament.* Examine your conscience in depth. Reflect on how you lived the virtues in the course of the day. Consider the roots of your flaws. Above all, focus on the things you must change (your values and your character), not on things you need not and probably cannot change (your temperament).

   As we have seen, temperament does not lend itself to change. We cannot switch temperaments as we would a pair of shoes. If you are phlegmatic by nature, it is absurd to try to act as if you were naturally passionate. Work on your character instead. As you grow in virtue, your personality will stabilize and the rough edges will be smoothed out.

C. *Be objective.* We achieve true self-knowledge only by encountering God. Put yourself in God's presence and ask, "Who are You?" And then, "Who am I?" Only in recognizing your fundamental relationship to God, along with your destiny and your vocation, do you see clearly what you need to change and who you need to become.

D. *Be concrete.* Don't bother asking yourself whether you are good or bad. Such general considerations lead nowhere. Instead call to mind your failures to practice virtue in the past 24 hours, and then set personal, concrete objectives for tomorrow.

SPIRITUAL DIRECTION

We are accustomed to turn to all manner of gurus and savants, not to mention lawyers, plumbers, beauticians, and fitness trainers, to help us to improve in some way or render us services we feel we cannot do without. And we are glad to pay top dollar to get what they have to offer.

Psychiatrists offer a useful service if the nature of what ails us is truly psychiatric. But where do you go if you want to *put your soul in order* and feel you cannot do it yourself? (You're right, you can't.) You go to a spiritual director.

Fundamental self-improvement without a spiritual director is highly unlikely to take place.

A spiritual director helps us overcome our fifth obstacle— the tendency to go easy on ourselves. A director will remove our illusions and give us orientation in our daily quest. Without his expert guidance, we risk spinning our wheels.

The first time you heard your own voice on a tape recorder, you probably could not believe it was you. The realization that that is how you sound to others very likely came as a shock. Just as we may be shocked at seeing a candid photo that shows us as we really look.

This salutary shock of recognition is what good spiritual direction provides. The director is the camera, the tape recorder, showing you to yourself as you really are. It may be a shock, but you need it. You are seeking moral and spiritual excellence. This requires pulling up defects root and branch. But first you need to know who you really are. The director will help you find out.

Escrivá says: "You think you are really somebody: your studies—your research, your publications; your social position; your name; your political accomplishments—the offices you hold; your wealth; your age . . . no longer a child. Precisely because of all of this, you—more than others— need a director for your soul."[2]

Be sincere. Lose your fear of appearing as you really are. Be obedient to your director's promptings.

To find the right director, practice what on Wall Street is called "due diligence." Do your homework. Exercise as much prudence and care as you would in selecting a spouse or choosing the right college for your 16-year-old.

The director should be someone you know to be an objective judge of character, with a reputation for virtuous behavior. It could be a friend, but it should never be your spouse. "A prudent loving friendship," says Pieper, "which is the sine qua non for genuine spiritual guidance, has nothing in common with sentimental intimacy, and indeed is rather imperiled by such intimacy."[3]

Through your local church or synagogue, perhaps, or through family members or a close friend, seek out an advisor of wisdom, maturity, and deep piety.

---

2. J. Escrivá, *The Way*, no. 63.
3. J. Pieper, *Prudence*. p. 56.

And then—what do you do in spiritual direction? Father John McCloskey, a Catholic priest with many years of experience working with professional men and women, says this about spiritual direction: "What do you talk about? Lots of things or very few. You can set the ground rules with the director. There should be an effort to address a very particular area of life, which needs improvement, that defect or fault that keeps you from making more rapid progress. And, oh yes, from time to time you may simply need to unburden yourself of unexpected joys and sorrows that come on your pilgrimage to the house of God, the Father."[4]

Father McCloskey recommends consulting with a spiritual director at least monthly, and preferably weekly or biweekly. Meetings need not last long. It is good to write down notes and resolutions dealing with points of improvement. Pray about the resolutions, put them into practice, and discuss them at your next meeting. Never leave one meeting without making an appointment for the next one.

Ernesto Cofiño, a prominent Latin American pediatrician, made regular spiritual direction part of his *plan of life*. He wrote of his experience: "With a loving hand my spiritual director was hewing the shapeless stone which I happened to be, with a sole advantage: I was pleased to be hewed, I enjoyed seeing the edges and corners of my character falling away. In fact, I was not aware of the figure that was coming out, but I had faith in the sculptor."[5]

---

4. Fr. J. McCloskey, "A Spiritual Consultant," on-line article, *SperoNews* (www.spero forum.com), Monday, November 28, 2005.
5. See J.L. Cofiño and J.M. Cejas, *Ernesto Cofiño*. Madrid: Rialp, 2003, p. 124.

PLAN OF LIFE

Examination of conscience and spiritual direction are part and parcel of a larger "plan of life." This plan begins with the idealistic desire to serve God and all his creatures completely and at all times, and takes shape in a very practical program for growing in virtue and, yes, in sanctity.

It's a question of regular spiritual exercises throughout the day—15 minutes of prayer (conversation with God), attendance at Divine Liturgy, including frequent reception of the Holy Eucharist, acts of self-denial, regular confession of sins, and praying for divine help to Mary, the Mother of God, by reciting the Rosary or other Marian prayers.

For those not accustomed to *practicing* their faith with such intensity, living a plan of life will be a considerable challenge. This plan of life is an excellent topic to take up with your spiritual director. Taking into account the state of your formation and the circumstances of your daily life, he will advise you on what you can realistically do to practice your faith more conscientiously.

A plan of life is a means to help you achieve union with God—it is not, and should never become, an end in itself. Escrivá says: "You should not let them become rigid rules, or water-tight compartments. They should be flexible, to help you on your journey, you who live in the middle of the world, with a life of hard professional work and social ties and obligations which you should not neglect, because in them your conversation with God still continues. Your plan of life ought to be like a rubber glove that fits the hand perfectly.

"Please don't forget that the important thing does not lie in doing many things; limit yourself, generously, to those you can fulfill each day, whether or not you happen to feel like doing them. These pious practices will lead you, almost without your realizing it, to contemplative prayer. Your soul will pour forth more acts of love, aspirations, acts of thanksgiving, acts of atonement, spiritual communions. And this will happen while you go about your ordinary duties, when you answer the telephone, get onto a bus, open or close a door, pass in front of a church, when you begin a new task, during it and when you have finished it: *you will find yourself referring everything you do to your Father God.*[6]

This last point is vital. The grace obtained in living a plan of life should spill over into the fulfillment of our ordinary responsibilities. That means living each moment of the day heroically: rising punctually and not lingering in bed after the alarm goes off, working conscientiously without daydreaming or killing time, avoiding the temptation of doing the agreeable task first and putting off the one we don't like, finishing a job as well as possible, correcting subordinates (charitably) even if we find this hard, sticking to our scheduled time of prayer even if we are thoroughly distracted or have no taste for it and feel we are getting nothing out of it, being friendly to people we are not terribly fond of, smiling when it's the last thing we feel like doing, putting up cheerfully with setbacks great and small, playing with the kids when we get home even if we're dead tired, eating what is put in front of us even if it's not to our liking, and generally being bearers of the light of Christ at all times and in all places.

If we have learned to do these things, we have achieved the greatest victory possible.

---

6. J. Escrivá, *Friends of God*, no. 149.

EPILOGUE

SOLZHENITSYN ONCE MUSED: "If only there were evil people somewhere insidiously committing evil deeds, and it were necessary only to separate them from the rest of us and destroy them. But the line dividing good and evil cuts through the heart of every human being, and who is willing to destroy his own heart?"

With his unerring strategic eye, Solzhenitsyn zoomed in on the essence of the matter—the human heart.

Those who would convert their hearts are the leaders. Those who would rather not are the also-rans.

To be a leader is to be eternally dissatisfied with one's self. Leaders are always in motion, on the way, changing. They strive to improve throughout their lives.

Leadership does not exclude anyone. It is the vocation not of the few but of the many. It may or may not involve fame, but it always involves virtue or it is not authentic leadership. It is always within our grasp. It is what God expects of us, and He does not set us up to fail.

Virtue contributes powerfully to success in professional and personal life but it does not guarantee it. In fact, it may bring ostracism (Solzhenitsyn, Escrivá, Lejeune) or even death (Stolypin, More, Joan of Arc).

But it will surely make you a beacon to those who know and love you and follow the trail you have blazed. How true the words of Escrivá: "In the constant practice of repeated self-denial in little things . . . with God's grace you will increase in strength of character. In that way, you'll first become master of yourself, and then a guide and leader: to compel, to urge, to draw with your example and with your word and with your knowledge and with your authority."[1]

Yes, the fruitful combination of humility ("deny yourself in little things"), self-control ("become master of yourself"), and magnanimity (". . . and then a guide and leader"): *this is* leadership—*virtuous* leadership!

Let me conclude with a piece of advice drawn from my own experience. If at times your failings lead you to despair and you feel you cannot continue in your quest, remind yourself of these words of Sacred Scripture: "With men it is impossible but not with God; for with God all things are possible."[2]

---

1. J. Escrivá, *The Way*, no. 19.
2. Mk 10:17–29.